PRACTICAL PSYCHOLOGY FOR POLICE OFFICERS

■ PRACTICAL ■
PSYCHOLOGY FOR
POLICE OFFICERS

By

MARTIN REISER, Ed. D.

Department Psychologist
Los Angeles Police Department

With a Foreword by

EDWARD M. DAVIS

Chief of Police
Los Angeles Police Department

CHARLES C THOMAS · PUBLISHER
Springfield · Illinois · U.S.A.

Published and Distributed Throughout the World by
CHARLES C THOMAS • PUBLISHER
Bannerstone House
301-327 East Lawrence Avenue, Springfield, Illinois, U.S.A.

© *1973, by* CHARLES C THOMAS • PUBLISHER
ISBN 0-398-02846-X
Library of Congress Catalog Card Number: 73-4208

Library of Congress Cataloging in Publication Data
Reiser, Martin, 1927-
  Practical psychology for police officers.
  1. Psychology. 2. Criminal psychology. 3. Police
psychology. I. Title.
[DNLM: 1. Crime. 2. Criminal psychology. 3. Psy-
chology. HV 6080 R375p 1973]
BF131.R365 363.2'01'9 73-4208 ISBN 0-398-02846-X

Printed in the United States of America
P-4

To the officers and staff of the Los Angeles Police Department who helped educate me about the police profession.

ACKNOWLEDGMENTS

I AM APPRECIATIVE of the strong support and cooperation of Chief Edward M. Davis and the Board of Police Commissioners.

My colleagues in the Personnel and Training Bureau have aided immeasurably, providing congeniality and expertise: Deputy Chief Norman L. Rector, Commanders Clifford J. Shannon and Thomas E. King, Lieutenants Jerold M. Bova and Joe W. Kinder, and Sergeant John W. Bangs III.

Robert J. Sokol, M.D., psychiatric consultant and friend, has contributed ideas and inspiration over the past four years.

Miss Susan Saxe, my assistant, has helped to lighten the daily burden, and my secretary, Miss Rachael Burrescia, agreeably took on the extra task of typing the final draft.

My wife, Enid, has been indispensable in this as in numerous other projects. Her encouragement and help are deeply appreciated.

Acknowledgment is also made to Karl Menninger, M.D., coauthors, and The Viking Press, publisher of *The Vital Balance*, for use of materials on the levels of dysfunction. Appreciation is also extended to John P. Spiegel, M.D., for use of his concepts on violence and riots.

FOREWORD

D R. MARTIN REISER has been Department Psychologist with the Los Angeles Police Department since the position was first filled in 1968. He brought to the police service his extensive background in clinical psychology and has applied that experience to the special needs of police officers and the police profession.

Dr. Reiser has taken on a difficult and sorely needed task with his new book. The text is generally intended for police officers. In that respect, it will fill a long standing void. The discussion of many previously undeveloped subjects by a professional psychologist will provide an insight much needed in the police profession. For too long, the police administrator has had to rely upon himself and his command staff to enforce high standards and discipline in his agency without the aid and practical support from behavioral scientists experienced with the unique problems of the police service. Marty Reiser's book should be a welcome reinforcement.

Moreover, the lay reader will find this book a refreshing look at a subject which has been on many people's minds—America's policemen. Dr. Reiser has taken a look at the police profession and the police officer from a sympathetic point of view, not with simply a clinical eye. Though he has done that too. Marty likes policemen (his brother is one) and policemen like him. The relationship has been mutually profitable.

The interested reader should receive a healthy insight into a subject which is all too often heavy with stereotyped images. Perhaps it will help to create a greater climate of understanding between our citizens and the officers who serve them.

Several years of practical experience with the Los Angeles Police Department have afforded Dr. Martin Reiser a unique experience to apply his profession's expertise to the police service.

He brought with him great perceptivity and unusual common sense, so important in dealing with the problems which the police service must face. His text should be a valuable contribution to the literature in his field as well as to the policeman's world.

E. M. DAVIS
Chief of Police
Los Angeles Police Department

PREFACE

A LTHOUGH THERE EXISTS a staggering array of clinical and theoretical writings on psychology, relatively little has been written specifically for police officers.

This book is not intended as a comprehensive text of scientific psychology. It is an attempt to present in plain language practical information of interest and value to law enforcement personnel.

This effort is an outgrowth of several years of unique and invaluable experience as psychologist for the Los Angeles Police Department.

Though the focus of this book was shaped by interactions with recruits, senior officers, specialists and police administrators, the points of view expressed are solely my responsibility.

MARTIN REISER

CONTENTS

PRACTICAL PSYCHOLOGY FOR POLICE OFFICERS

CHAPTER ONE

WHAT ARE POLICEMEN

REALLY LIKE?

THE POLICE OFFICER in today's society is an executive.[14]
He functions relatively independently with minimal supervision in stress situations requiring high-level decision-making
and expertise. As an expert in the *people business,* he can no
longer be dismissed with the old stereotype of brawn rather than
brains. He is aware that his is a knowledge occupation where
the *how to* approach must increasingly be augmented by the *why*
of behavior. As a consequence, educational emphases in police
departments have been shifting toward the behavioral sciences,
humanities and liberal arts from a narrowly specialized tech-
nological orientation. However, the many-sided questions about
the priorities and dimensions of the policeman's role are far from
completely answered. That is understandable since the role is
constantly in the process of evolving.

THE POLICEMAN'S ROLE

The policeman's role is multiplex. In a very real sense the
policeman in the community is a man in the middle. He is caught
and must function between the existing written law and the
rapidly changing values of the community. He must not only
confront and comprehend complex social issues, but also must
deal with a variety of subcultures which are clashing with each
other and which are also in conflict internally. In order to function as an effective professional, the modern police officer must
have some working knowledge of human psychology. Understanding people and cool headedness are two of the character-

3

istics most frequently mentioned in connection with the policeman's role.[40]

Charged by the citizens of the community to uphold and enforce the laws, the policeman is also expected to use discretion and wisdom in handling sensitive or ambiguous situations.

The professional police officer is actually a combination of specialists rolled into one. He functions in part as a psychologist, lawyer, mediator, teacher, criminologist and public relations expert. In addition, he also represents the local government since he is the most visible public official. He must represent all of the people equally and fairly in whichever of the specialist roles he happens to be functioning at the time.

The police role today involves several main dimensions: peacekeeping, public service, law enforcement, and crime suppression and prevention. It has been estimated that the peacekeeping and service responsibilities of the police officer occupy approximately eighty percent of his total time.[22] This includes mediating family disturbances, looking for lost children, taking reports, giving directions, etc.[39]

Although there is still a point of view that arresting criminals is the sole legitimate function of the police officer, the current and future reality is that police work is primarily a service occupation. A policeman can view this fact of life as either demeaning or as former Police Chief William H. Parker has put it, *Public service is one of the noblest professions.*[47]

Law enforcement and combating crime occupies an important but smaller amount of the average policeman's time. However, the problems of crime and processing of criminals have become increasingly unwieldy because of the many inadequacies in the larger criminal justice system. Emphasis on early parole and probation but inadequate screening by behavioral specialists of persons convicted of serious crime has resulted in a revolving door situation where criminals are apprehended by the police one day and are back in business or reapprehended a short time later. This situation compounds the frustration and represents poor economy in effecting the law enforcement function of the police officer.

To ameliorate this situation, a systems approach will be necessary wherein each sub-system of the criminal justice network including police, judiciary, probation, and corrections will have to address itself not only to its own unique area of responsibility but also to its relationships to the other sub-systems as well. Because the corrections sub-system has been relatively ineffectual in rehabilitating persons convicted of serious crime, a new infusion of behavioral science expertise and programming would seem very desirable.

Potentially, the policeman has most significant impact in the crime prevention area because prevention involves a long range program affecting attitudes, character traits and behavior. By being available as a positive, adequate model for children and others to identify with, and by setting the proper example, police officers can have considerable influence on the development of value systems and behavioral norms. Although prevention in police work has been given lip service for many years, relatively little has actually been done to come to grips with the many possibilities that exist. In developing approaches to prevention, the behavioral scientist familiar with child development and the multiple influences on character building should be involved.

Over the years the police officer has been poorly paid and also relegated to an unprofessional status. This in contrast to the expectations of society that police officers perform as highly competent professionals. Nationwide, the police service has been upgrading itself through education, selection and training. But it is actually the citizens and society who determine whether the policeman role will have professional status by providing adequate compensation and recognition of the high level skills required.

INTELLIGENCE, EMOTIONAL STABILITY AND MOTIVATION

Police work is one of the very few occupations that often require an initial evaluation including written, background, physical and psychological assessments. This amounts to a filtering process where only those who pass through the preceding screens can continue on to qualify for appointment as a policeman. In large urban police departments perhaps ten percent of those who take the initial written test get through the various screening phases to the appointment list. It should be no surprise that the overwhelming majority of research reports on policemen populations utilizing psychological testing and assessment reveal that, in general, policemen tested are above average: in intelligence, in emotional stability, in ability to get along with people, and in the desire to serve the community.[4, 8, 28, 44] For example, a factorial description of the composite policeman's profile by psychologist Raymond Cattell says,

> They adaptively fit the needs of practical alertness and decisiveness, toughness in difficulties, emotional stability, identification with moral standards in the job. Traditionally one notes from second order factor scores decidedly below average anxiety and neuroticism and a temperament which makes contact with people easier.[10]

A research study by psychologist Jay Gottesman using the Minnesota Multiphasic Personality Inventory concluded that, "The mean police applicant MMPI Profile is helpful and 'more normal' than that of the control group."[18] Another study by psychologist Robert B. Mills and associates using a psychological test battery, situational tests and interviews concluded, "Police officers on the whole, are a psychologically healthy group who do not differ greatly from the so-called 'normal' group."[24] Psychologist Ruth Levy found the large sample of policemen tested had a better than average ability to handle stress.[22]

Another study by psychologist Joseph Matarazzo found his successful policeman group at the *very healthy end of each scale.* They had strong needs to achieve and to excel, be the center of attention, understand and dominate others, do a job until done, and be one of the boys. They also like to work with others, needing little kindness from others and giving little sympathy. They felt little animosity or aggression toward their fellow men.[23]

A recent research study done by specialists at the University of Chicago outlines some ideal traits for success as a patrolman. These attributes were all related to stability: stability in the parental and personal family situation, stability stemming from personal self-confidence and the control of emotional impulses, stability in the maintenance of cooperative rather than hostile attitudes, and stability derived from a resistance to stress and a realistic rather than a subjective orientation toward life.[4]

Three of the main motives of men selecting the police profession today are action, recognition and responsibility. These individuals are action-oriented and like to be where things are happening. They are also motivated by a need for recognition and for high achievement. Responsibility as a motive is seen in the desire to serve the community, to maintain the standards of society, to utilize constructive approaches to problem-solving.

In the past, applicants to police work were primarily motivated by their security needs including salary, structure, and civil service tenure. However, over the years there has been a shift in the need hierarchy with the desire to contribute to community life rating highest while financial and job security motives rate farther down on the scale.[38]

SELF-IMAGE, IDENTIFICATION AND SECURITY

Man is his own worst enemy. He puts blinders on and locks chains around himself. He then limps through life rather than running on all cylinders. He doubts his abilities, fears making a decision and feels tension and anxiety about facing new situations.

A person's inner security is based on his image of himself as a person, his self-concept. If he feels good about himself, worthwhile and valuable, he will tend to see himself as grown-up and equal to all other adults. If he feels inadequate, guilty, and doubts his worth, he will feel insecure and childlike. In addition, he will feel helpless to cope with the harsh cruel world. This leads to cynicism and depression.

The nature of one's sexual identification is a key factor in the kind of self-concept one develops. If a person has had good models to identify with in growing up, with praise and positive discipline rather than constant criticism and belittling, he will probably feel comfortable and secure in his male role.

However, apart from early childhood influences, there are influences on the job which can also help shape a person's confidence and self-image.

The "John Wayne" Syndrome

This is a condition in which the individual tends to swagger and talk tough. He is somewhat badge-heavy in manner, feels that emotion is unhealthy and tends to keep his feelings locked inside under tight control. He feels he must always be right and cannot admit his fallibility or making a mistake. The philosophy is to shoot from the hip and ask questions later.

He tends to maintain the double standard, with women being seen as inferior. Women are divided into two distinct categories, either pure and asexual, like mother, or sexual and dirty like the prostitute. He puts the *pure* woman on a pedestal and adopts a worshipful but distant attitude. He can now strive toward and long for but never really attain equality with her. The sexual *ruined* woman is seen as debased and inferior since she has fallen from grace.

Because of his distorted attitudes toward women, he finds it difficult to establish a close, warm relationship with a female partner. Underneath the tough facade the individual presents to the world is considerable insecurity, self-doubt, and a shaky masculine image.

Inner Versus Outer Controls

The mature adult is largely directed by his own value system. In the process of growing up, he has internalized certain prohibitions, limits and moral values which affect his behavior later as an adult. If he contravenes these taboos, he develops guilt feelings. As an inner-directed person he doesn't need a policeman outside to reinforce his sense of right and wrong to prevent him from acting on impulse. He regulates his own actions.

The mature police officer who has a viable inner control system doesn't need an Internal Affairs Division to make him follow the proper procedures with citizens, suspects and fellow officers. He does what is ethical because of his own value system. The individual who needs constant outside controls is immature. However, a good inner control system does not imply emotional rigidity or coldness. It means having access to feelings and the ability to express them appropriately in particular situations. Self-acceptance results in being at ease with one's feelings and in less inner conflict over maintaining self-control.

Professional Versus Personal Reactions

The professional police officer is self-confident because he has a positive self-concept. He sees himself as a person in a profession, with objectivity and the ability to step back for an impersonal look in handling emotionally loaded situations with citizens and suspects.

He is able to differentiate between his role as a professional and his own personal feelings with the awareness that personal reactions to the job are usually inappropriate. Therefore, when he is provoked by a hostile, antagonistic suspect on the street, he knows this is a result of the suspect's insecurity and inadequacy.

Rather than allowing himself to be manipulated into a knockdown, drag-out fight so the suspect can prove to the officer that he is a bigger man, the officer asks himself the key question, *Whose problem is it?* The answer is that it is the suspect's problem. He can then sympathize with the suspect for having serious identity conflicts, but calmly goes about completing the transaction.

Taunts, name-calling, blustering, and other kinds of provocative behaviors are understood by the professional officer as symptoms of insecurity and not really his problem. However, if he is physically attacked, the professional officer uses whatever minimum force is necessary to contain the suspect.

Developing a professional attitude requires experience and the ability to discriminate one's own from someone else's feelings and reactions. By a process of self-examination, the professional can distinguish which of his feelings are based on personal emotional biases and which responses are oriented toward getting the job done effectively with the least amount of strain.

Authority Versus Authoritarianism

The professional policeman has an attitude of authority. He is calm, objective and self-confident with the main focus on getting the job done most efficiently. Because of his training, experience and self-regard, he communicates an image of knowledgeability and mature helpfulness. He is not passive, wishy-washy, or continually doubting himself. On the other hand, he does not assume an attitude of omnipotence and invulnerability, but goes about his task with dispatch and efficiency, recognizing that he can make mistakes and admit to them.

The authoritarian personality, on the other hand, tends to be prejudiced and overly aggressive toward people belonging to minority groups. In order to feel superior to other people, he stereotypes and labels them. In addition to his exaggerated need to prove his strength and toughness, the authoritarian individual has generalized hostility and a tendency to look down on others. He is also narrow-minded and rigid in his thinking.

In past research on authoritarianism, these traits have been grouped under the heading of *ethnocentrism* which is a kind of provincialism and cultural narrowness. The term *ethnocentrism* refers to group relations generally as compared with the term *prejudice,* which is normally defined as a dislike against a specific group.[33]

Comparing attitudes of authority to authoritarianism, it should be noted that authority is related to self-worth, self-confidence, a liking for people and a sense of balance and flexibility. Authoritarianism is related to close-mindedness, insecurity about one's basic worth, need to feel superior and to see things narrowly as either good or bad, black or white. There is also an inability to tolerate any uncertainty or ambiguity.

Suspiciousness—The Trained Observer

Policemen are often stereotyped as paranoid, overly suspicious and apprehensive about people's motives. However, it is important to differentiate between the characteristics required of the trained observer and those which reflect a personal conflict or disturbance.

Professionals in the various helping occupations need to observe in detail verbal and non-verbal kinds of behavior in order to make useful and valid assessments about what they are dealing with. The manner in which a person says something, the tone of voice, the body posture, the facial expression, the avoidance of certain topics, the sequence in which particular words are used or are omitted, all have significance in evaluating a particular situation. Mental health professionals, teachers, lawyers and others utilize these important clues on a day-to-day basis in their work with little conflict and without being accused of having questionable motives.

The police professional, however, although he too must be a trained observer if he is to discover, suppress or arrest crime, is often criticized in this regard. Explaining the job requirements for policemen to the public is only partially effectual. However, the experience of riding in a patrol car in a high crime area would enable the citizen to discover the real need for vigilance and close observation on the part of the officer. The author can personally attest to the effectiveness of this experience.

Like many of my colleagues and other citizens, prior to becoming familiar with police work and its demands, I tended to have a blind spot in regard to the role and functions of the police officer. I was unconcerned, usually tuning-out occurrences on the street which might involve an argument, a fight, a drunk, or a robbery because they didn't fit in with my role at the time. After riding around in patrol cars for numerous hours, I felt my perceptions and attitudes changing considerably.

In the police car, I found there was a specific job focus and requirement imposed on you, observing, discovering crime, and being aware of events and clues which might suggest harm or danger to someone. I became much more aware and observant of what goes on in a liquor store at night, in a dark alley, and what's happening in a mob scene.[30] These are bread and butter reality problems for the police officer which he is required to pay attention to. Without close attention to these details, he is not doing his job adequately.

The suspiciousness of the policeman is an absolute necessity if he is to be effective in his role. In his contact with and exposure to a variety of individuals who are violent or dishonest the policeman soon learns the fact of life that everyone cannot be accepted at face value. He has to look beneath the surface for the person's motives, and pay attention to all of the available clues before arriving at a conclusion.

Like the psychologist, the police officer learns to quickly make a global assessment of people in a particular situation rather than accepting a simplistic answer or a nonsensical reason for an event. Because of his frequent involvement with a small segment of the population involved in illegal and socially proscribed activities, there is a danger of his assuming that all people are dishonest or untrustworthy.

The professional police officer is on guard against overgeneralizing and developing this kind of tunnel vision. By maintaining friends outside of his occupational group, continuing his education, and by knowing that a variety of views in society is healthy, he keeps an open mind and an even balance.

BIBLIOGRAPHY

1. Abbatiello, A.: *A Study of Police Candidate Selection*. Presented at the American Psychological Association Convention, Washington, D.C., 1969.
2. Adorno, T. W. et al: *The Authoritarian Personality*, Vols. 1 & 2. Somerset, Wiley, 1964.
3. Allport, Gordon: *The Nature of Prejudice*. Los Angeles, Anch. Doubleday, 1958.
4. Baehr, Melany et al: *Psychological Assessment of Patrolman Qualifications in Relation to Field Performance*. Washington, D.C. Law Enforcement Assistance Administration Project #046, November, 1968.
5. Banton, Michael: *The Policeman in the Community*. New York, Basic, 1964.
6. Becker, Harold and Felkenes, George: *Law Enforcement—A Selected Bibliography*. Metuchen, Scarecrow, 1968.
7. Bittner, Egon: *The Functions of the Police in Modern Society*. National Institute of Mental Health, November, 1970.
8. Blum, Richard: *Police Selection*. Springfield, Thomas, 1964.
9. Bordua, David (ed.): *The Police: Six Sociological Essays*. Somerset, Wiley, 1967.
10. Cattell, Raymond E.: *Factor Description of Composite Policeman's Profile*. Institute for Personality and Ability Testing. Champaign, 1967.
11. Chevigny, Paul: *Police Power*. New York, Pantheon, 1969.
12. Clark, Ramsey: *Crime in America*. New York, S. & S., 1970.
13. Doig, J. W.: The police in a democratic society. *Public Administration Review*, September-October, 1968.
14. Drucker, Peter: Personal Communication Seminar, L.A.P.D., December 16, 1971.
15. Durkheim, Emile: *Professional Ethics and Civil Morals*. Routledge and Kegan Paul, 1957.
16. Eilbert, Leo R.: *Research on the Selection of Police Recruits*. American Institutes for Research, August, 1966.

17. Goldstein, Leo: Perspectives on law enforcement: Characteristics of police applicants. Princeton, Educational Testing Service, June, 1970.

18. Gottesman, Jay: *Personality Patterns of Urban Police Applicants as Measured by the MMPI.* Hoboken, Stevens Institute of Technology, September, 1969.

19. Hankey, Richard: *Personality Correlation in a Role of Authority: The Police.* Unpublished Doctoral Dissertation, University of Southern California, 1968.

20. Lamb, H. Richard: *Police Professionalization—a Central Focus for Mental Health Consultation.* Presented at American Psychiatric Association Convention, May, 1970.

21. *Law and Order Reconsidered.* Staff Report, National Commission on the Cause and Prevention of Violence. U.S. Government Printing Office, 1969.

22. Levy, Ruth: Predicting police failure. *Journal of Criminal Law, Criminology and Police Science,* 58:275:1967.

23. Matarazzo, Joseph D. et al: Characteristics of successful policemen and firemen applicants. *Journal of Applied Psychology,* Vol. 48, No. 2, April, 1964.

24. Mills, Robert B.: Use of diagnostic small groups in police recruit selection. *Journal of Criminal Law, Criminology and Police Science,* Vol. 60, No. 2, June, 1969.

25. Niederhoffer, A. and Blumberg, A. S.: *The Ambivalent Force: Perspectives on the Police.* Waltham, Ginn College, 1970.

26. O'Rourke, William J.: Should all policemen be college trained? *The Police Chief,* December, 1971, pp. 36-38.

27. Packer, Herbert: *The Limits of Criminal Sanction.* Stanford, Stanford U. Press, 1968.

28. Petersen, Margaret et al.: Psychiatric screening of Policemen. Presented at Midwest Meeting of the American Psychiatric Association, November, 1968.

29. Reiser, Martin: On origins of hatred toward Negroes. In Levitas, G. B. (ed.): *The World of Psychoanalysis,* New York, Braziller, 1965.

30. Reiser, Martin: A psychologist's view of the badge. *Police Chief,* September, 1970, pp. 24-26.

31. Reiser, Martin: *The Police Department Psychologist.* Springfield, Thomas, 1972.

32. Reiser, Martin and Steinberg, J. L.: *To Protect and Serve: An Information Guide for Police Officers to Increase Effectiveness in the Community.* Los Angeles Police Department, 1971.

33. Rokeach, Milton: *Beliefs, Attitudes and Values.* San Francisco, Jossey-Bass, 1968.

34. Schrag, Clarence: *Crime and Justice: American Style.* Center for Studies of Crime and Delinquency, NIMH, 1971.

35. Singer, H. A.: The cop as social scientist. *The Police Chief*, April, 1970, pp. 52-58.
36. Skolnick, Jerome: *Justice Without Trial*. Somerset, Wiley, 1966.
37. Smith, Bruce: *Police Systems in the United States*. New York, Harp T., 1960.
38. Sterling, James W.: *Changes in Role Concepts of Police Officers*. International Association of Chiefs of Police, 1972.
39. *Task Force Report: The Police*. The President's Commission on Law Enforcement and the Administration of Justice. U.S. Government Printing Office, 1967.
40. *The Challenge of Crime in a Free Society*. The President's Commission on Law Enforcement and the Administration of Justice. U.S. Government Printing Office, 1967.
41. *The Urban Police Function*. American Bar Association Project on Standards for Criminal Justice, March, 1972.
42. *To Establish Justice, to Insure Domestic Tranquility*. Final Report of the National Commission on the Causes and Prevention of Violence. U.S. Government Printing Office, 1969.
43. Turner, William: *The Police Establishment*. New York, Putnam, 1968.
44. Walther, Regis H.: The psychological dimensions of work. Mimeo, January, 1970.
45. Wetteroth, William: The Psychological Training and Education of New York City Policemen. Presented at American Psychological Association Convention, Washington, D.C., September, 1971.
46. Whitaker, Ben: *The Police*. Baltimore, Penguin, 1964.
47. Wilson, James Q.: *Varieties of Police Behavior*. Cambridge, Harvard U. Press, 1968.
48. Wilson, O. W.: *Parker on Police*. Springfield, Thomas, 1957.
49. Wilson, O. W.: *Police Planning*, 2nd ed. Springfield, Thomas, 1958.

CHAPTER TWO

PERSONAL STRESS AND OCCUPATIONAL HAZARDS

A LONG WITH PSYCHIATRY, air traffic controlling, space engineering and test piloting, police work is a stress occupation. This involves a more than average amount of stress on a day-to-day basis compared to other occupations. By being aware of the sources of stress and of some typical problems that are related to it, a police officer can be prepared to deal with the problem more effectively and to utilize constructive defenses.

PROBLEMS OF NEW POLICEMEN

The challenges and difficulties facing a man new to police work are different from those the experienced officer encounters. This applies to men in other occupations as well since a process of adaptation to the new and unfamiliar is necessary in any situation.

Some Changing Attitudes

The young recruits coming into the police academy are typically very idealistic and interested in actively doing something constructive about the variety of social problems affecting society. However, over a period of time, the original idealism gets modified because of job pressures from a variety of sources, peer influences and organizational shaping effects. The original idealism may become diluted by an overriding need for pragmatism and an attitude of cynicism.

The recruit's concept of himself undergoes some modification as those attributes in his value system change along with his new identification as a police officer. He may see himself as opposed to and disliking people and behavior that were previously conflict free.

Because of high stress and the impact of multiple aggressive and hostile encounters, and because he represents a negative authority symbol to many people, he may tend to defend himself by over-simplifying. People are then dichotomized into two groups, the good guys and the bad guys. Complex issues are decided as either black or white. The utility of labeling things in a simplistic fashion is in not expending the energy, time and uncertainty involved in dealing with ambiguity.

There may also be changes in attitude toward wife and family. As he becomes more immersed in his work and begins to identify strongly with his more experienced peers on the department, the new policeman may feel a kind of competition between the family and his job.

He is convinced his first loyalty should be toward his job. This conviction tends to get reinforced by the ethic that he is on duty twenty-four hours a day, and therefore, must maintain his mantle of professionalism and responsibility at all times. He then finds it harder to hang-up his policeman role away from the job and to shift to the person role in the family situation.

A Developmental Profile

The new young recruit is somewhat like a sponge. He idealistically soaks up the philosophy, techniques and *good stuff* that he is taught at the academy. He starts out with eagerness, a desire to maintain society's positive values and to do a first-rate job as taught.

During his academy training he has been under considerable stress and tension in keeping up academically, in passing the tough physical training program, and in merely making it through a demanding and difficult recruit program. However, his early optimistic attitudes frequently change after he is assigned to the field.

One of the things the recruit is often told when he reaches his first assignment is to "Forget the crap they taught you at the academy, we'll teach you what police work is really like." Thus, an intense conflict is created within the recruit between the idealism he started with and his need to be accepted in his new assignment.

Being told that his good training and ideals are unrealistic and not workable, causes feelings of disillusionment, resentment and uncertainty. However, in resolving his internal conflict and reducing his dissonance, he has only one workable choice open to him. He feels forced by peer pressure to adopt the attitudes, behaviors and standards of his training officers, supervisors and colleagues in his new division of assignment.

Going through this conflict leaves its mark on him. He learns to value more and more what is practical and pragmatic and to look down on things which are idealistic or ivory tower. He also starts becoming cynical because he has learned that things aren't what they seem to be.

Since he is still on probation for another six or seven months after his initial training, he must be very careful to please his training officers and supervisors in order to get good ratings and secure permanent tenure.

Over the next few years the new policeman is typically a go-getter, interested in making good arrests and putting bad guys in jail. He defends himself against complexity and ambiguity by developing a hard-headed, know-it-all attitude. Instructors in the in-service training courses for the two to four-year policeman class find it a very difficult group to impart information to. However, this in-group defensiveness does have a preservative function for young officers during this stage of their development. It counters stress, anxiety and danger.

After approximately five years of experience the young policeman typically begins to mellow. He learns to relax, to regain his sense of humor, to smile and joke with people again, and to not take himself so seriously. The years of experience with crises and handling them have taught him considerable poise and self-confidence. His former heightened defensiveness is no longer necessary. With this relaxation often comes a growing interest in the complexities of life outside of police work and a renewed interest in wife and family.

Being One of the Boys

There are many pressures on the new policeman to identify with peers as one of the boys. He feels increased strength in group cohesiveness and solidarity.

The potential danger in his working environment may discourage the policeman from outside friendships. This tends to isolate him from various segments of the community, not only those perceived as dangerous but also those with whom he could have some common interest. The feeling of social isolation and distance tends to reinforce the need for in-group values and sharing among policemen.[19] This is reflected in the statement, "Unless you are a policeman and have been there, you can't possibly understand what it is like."

Organizational Stress

In addition to the newness, uncertainty, and being the low man on the totem pole, the new policeman is also a member of a quasi-military organization which has additional influences on him.

The organizational philosophy and procedure may conflict with values the new policeman has brought with him from his own subculture. Because he reflects the society from which he comes and because large organizations by nature are monolithic and have many built-in resistances, he finds that when he asks why something is being done he may not get an adequate answer immediately or, he may be told to shut up, stop asking questions and just do it.

He is being inspected and evaluated persistently, not only by his supervisors but also by the public at large. As a representative of the organization, he is ever on display, constantly being judged. He also has to adjust to time and schedule demands, whether working longer and strange hours, or periodically changing his routine, requiring a complete readjustment for himself and his family.

In most organizations there are communication problems. It may be difficult to get opinions, feelings and gripes heard. If communication channels are inadequate, with messages going only from the top down, he will develop the common feeling that the *brass* don't know what's happening and don't really care about the man on the street.

The young policeman is interested in promotion and getting ahead in his new career. He very early becomes aware of the importance of avoiding punishment by Division sanctions or a Board of Rights. He also learns that the police department has its own internal investigation division whose job it is to police the policeman. If he reacts negatively, this causes additional stress because he feels under surveillance, that he has to work and live in a glass cage.

Traditionally, promotions in police organizations are from the bottom up, over fixed intervals, to each succeeding level of command. This can be perceived as an obstacle to the individual with high achievement motives who feels he is being held back merely by time constraints and not allowed to demonstrate his abilities as rapidly as he feels capable of doing.

HAZARDS ON THE JOB

In addition to the stresses and pressures emanating from within himself and from the organization, the police officer has to contend with additional real threats and dangers while he is working daily.

Danger—You Can Get Killed Out There

Although mining and farming are statistically more dangerous occupations, police work has become increasingly hazardous. In discussing the working environment of the policeman, Skolnick states that the two main variables involved in police work which create constant pressure are danger and authority.[25] Danger affectively shapes the policeman to be especially attentive to potentially violent situations.

As community values and attitudes change, increased militancy, outspokenness and expression of feelings through actions become more commonplace. This results in a significant increase in aggressive and hostile acting-out behavior. This trend is reflected in statistical figures of assaults on policemen.

In 1970, a total of 251,955 people were arrested by the police in the City of Los Angeles. While taking these people into custody, 1,529 policemen were assaulted with guns, knives, scalding liquid and caustic chemicals. During the year, 2,916 hand guns, shot guns, rifles and automatic weapons were destroyed along with 6,000 pounds of other deadly instruments.

To those social critics who advocate disarming the police, one can only reply that the policeman must work in a subculture of violence and is armed by necessity and by the realities of life in the community.

Nationally, in 1971, 125 local, county and state officers were murdered as compared with 100 officers slain in 1970. The F.B.I. reports that twenty officers died as a result of ambush-type attacks; twenty-four were killed responding to robbery calls; seven were answering burglary calls; twenty as a result of traffic stops; nine while handling disturbances; seven killed by mentally disturbed persons; twenty-two while making arrests; seven at the hands of prisoners; and nine were killed investigating suspicious persons or circumstances. Ninety-six percent of these killings were committed with firearms.[12]

In order to survive in an often hostile working environment and to achieve some modicum of effectiveness on the job, the police officer must successfully deal with the constant stress and pressure that is imposed on him. In addition to confronting real danger, the policeman also has to cope with the temptations that surround him constantly.

The Temptations—Sex, Alcohol and Money

It is well-known that many females find uniforms particularly alluring and attractive. This applies to military uniforms, waiters, doormen and, of course, policemen. If anything, the man in the police uniform is even more attractive because he represents the safe authority figure on the one hand, and the epitome of virility and manliness on the other.

Statistically, there is a preponderance of females to males in our society. Many women have been divorced, widowed, or have experienced unsatisfactory male-female relationships in the past. The old double standard has changed and women today are more expressive and willing to be aggressive and open about their sexual needs.

Because there are many attractive women available who find young policemen particularly desirable, the temptation to the officer to get involved in easy sexual liaisons has significantly increased. Converting an official contact into a personal one is one of the common charges leading to punitive action against officers. The resistance to temptation is related to maturity and the quality of one's personal life.

The Don Juan character who measures his virility by the number of women he goes to bed with, is subconsciously very insecure about his masculinity. The married policeman who is tempted into extramarital affairs by an attractive female largely for the sexual gratification is predictably insecure and dissatisfied with his marriage. The man who is sure of his maleness feels adequate sexually and has no need to prove himself a stud or sexual acrobat.

In some instances a pervasive sense of sexual inadequacy can be carried over from an early childhood feeling of having a small penis and therefore, not be able to satisfy a normal female sexually.[22] The fact is that the size of one's penis has very little bearing on sexual effectiveness or satisfaction for either partner. Consideration for the sexual needs of the female are important but the primary factor in achieving sexual compatibility is emotional warmth and closeness.

Alcohol

Like sex, alcohol can be used as an escape hatch when one is under stress, pressure and anxiety. Social drinking is an acceptable and relatively harmless activity in our society. Like most things, however, when it is overdone, it can become a serious problem.

Alcoholism is an affliction which typically crystallizes in middle age. It develops insidiously over ten to fifteen years and finally results in a well-established habit pattern with physiological as well as psychological dependencies on the drug. Current research has not proved genetic or biochemical reasons for the development of alcohol abuse. Although various physiological, psychological, and sociological theories have been advanced to account for alcoholism, to date, the findings are highly tentative. The most important factor probably involves learning. Some studies have indicated that among ethnic groups who use alcohol to a large degree, the lowest incidence of alcoholism is associated with certain behaviors and attitudes.[2, 3, 6]

1. The children are exposed to alcohol early in life, with a strong family or religious group. Whatever the beverage, it is served in very diluted form and in small quantities with consequent low blood-alcohol level.
2. The beverages commonly used by the groups are those containing large amounts of non-alcoholic components which also give low blood-alcohol levels.
3. The beverage is considered mainly as a food and is usually consumed with meals, again with subsequent low blood-alcohol levels.
4. Parents present a constant example of moderate drinking.
5. No moral importance is attached to drinking, which is considered neither a virtue nor a sin.
6. Drinking is not viewed as the proof of adulthood or virility.
7. Abstinence is socially acceptable. It is no more rude or ungracious to decline a drink than to decline a piece of bread.
8. Excessive drinking or intoxication is not socially acceptable. It is not considered stylish, comic or tolerable.
9. Finally, and perhaps most important, there is wide and usually complete agreement among the group on what might be called the ground rules of drinking.

Some common early warning signs of a developing drinking problem are the need to drink before facing certain situations, frequent drinking sprees, steadily increasing intake, solitary drinking, early morning drinking, Monday morning absenteeism, frequent disputes about drinking, and the occurrence of blackouts. A common misconception is that to be an alcoholic, one has to resemble the skid row character. Actually, individuals with this problem come from all socioeconomic levels of society.

Alcohol abuse may be related to basic emotional conflicts in the areas of overdependence and repressed hostility. Alcohol is often a crutch for the dependent individual. At the same time, it is also his way of getting even with others in the environment who he feels deprive him of love and acceptance.

Policemen frequently work in an environment where social and heavy drinking are commonplace. This may lead to the use of alcohol as a tranquillizer to reduce tension and anxiety. Over time, this seemingly common pattern may become a habit and then an addiction to alcohol.

Money

In some police jurisdictions accepting gratuities is considered a normal way of life by citizens and policemen alike. Obviously, this results in all kinds of problems including dishonesty, loss of personal integrity and unethical practices.

Policemen are like other people in having aspirations for achievement and living the good life. Society values the acquisition of the prerequisites of middle class America which includes property, gadgets and living up to advertised standards. Because the police officer traditionally has been paid poorly, he has found it difficult to achieve the standard of living to which he aspires. Therefore, the policeman who works two or more jobs is not uncommon. Upward mobility is part of the American dream.

There is considerable pressure to achieve the desired good life. Easy credit can lead to perpetual deficit financing with more outgo than income. If the consequence is dunning letters and other forms of creditor pressure, it becomes an official department problem which the individual policeman must answer for.

In some cases, the financial difficulties are more related to emotional conflicts in the marriage or to immaturity in one or both marital partners, making it difficult for them to face up to the daily responsibilities of budgeting and financial management. The inability to postpone, to plan for the future, and the impulsive *I must have it now* are common indicators of the financially immature attitude.

Police credit unions, banks and other financial organizations usually give free or low cost budgeting advice and financial management assistance to those who ask for it. The adult man admits he has a problem and seeks financial help before his job is in jeopardy.

Anger, Prejudice and Stereotypes

Much of the conflict that exists between men in police work and others in the community involves a large amount of underlying anger and resentment. Although many superficially logical reasons are given for the angry feelings, many of them are really rationalizations, because the underlying motives are usually unconscious and, therefore, outside of the person's awareness.

Policemen, like other people, are entitled to their private biases and personal feelings. However, because he is a professional, he can't allow his personal attitudes to adversely affect the way he approaches and deals with people on the job. For most people, what gives pleasure and is familiar tends to be comforting and reassuring. What is unfamiliar and unsatisfying tends to provoke fear and anxiety. This psychological principle is at work and has to be made conscious and considered in making judgments and in forming opinions.

Prejudices are pre-judgments in regard to situations or things that are unfamiliar or different. In interpersonal relationships we tend to defend ourselves against anxiety and the unfamiliar by adopting an attitude of superiority.

An intense, emotionally-based feeling of superiority about our own race, religion or ethnic group will influence our objectivity when we deal professionally with individuals who are ethnically different from ourselves. If extreme, it will make us incapable of adequately judging the significance of certain kinds of behavior which differ from the standards and practices of our own group.

An antidote to prejudice is openmindedness and the ability to tolerate uncertainty until the facts are in before arriving at a conclusion.

Stereotypes are images or labels based on exaggerated assumptions and having a large emotional charge. They are generalizations which automatically assign certain group characteristics to anyone who belongs to that group.

Although stereotyping may be economical from the standpoint of mental energy in that it requires less thought and effort, the lumping of people together under labels is inaccurate as well as unfair. It eliminates all of the individual differences that are bound to be present, in value system, religion, political and personal point of view.

Over the years, policemen have had extensive experience as a minority group being stereotyped by others. As a result, police officers should have greater sensitivity to this problem when dealing with other minority and *different* groups.

For eons people have been in conflict over power and status. We seem to need a pecking order to survive in group living. One reason for this is given by Storr.[27]

> Aggression is a drive as innate, as natural, and as powerful as sex. The theory that aggression is merely a response to frustration is no longer tenable in the light of biological research.

The Policeman As Authority Symbol

Traditionally humans have devised many emblems of authority such as the crown, the mace, the birch rod, the razor strap and the key to the executive washroom. The policeman's badge and gun are current emblems of authority.

Questions about who is in charge, and about territorial rights are as active today as ever. As we become more civilized, we have been able to evolve slightly from acting-out of impulses to the partial ability to symbolize them. However, individuals vary greatly in this regard. To the extent that underlying dependency conflicts are unresolved, there is a like amount of smoldering resentment, anger and rage pushing for expression.

> During our early development we are largely influenced by the surrounding environment. Particularly important is the harshness or lovingness of the significant people in our lives. At certain points very early we begin to internalize some of these external environmental influences and take them for our own. But because the early perceptual and cognitive apparatus is only partially developed, there tend to be large distortions and misperceptions of what is taken in. Thus, the early conscience which is the internal representation of environmental taboos and prohibitions, is frequently more harsh and atavistic than were the original external sources. This vengeful conscience is typical for early developmental levels but it should be softened and modified by subsequent life experiences and the

strengthening of one's self-image. However, in varying degrees some of this archaic conscience lingers on—an anachronism.

How do we deal with this punishing avenger inside of us? One defense is to gain distance from it. To do this we have to get rid of it by pushing it outside. A handy gimmick in this regard is the defense of projection. For this to work smoothly we need a hook to hang it on. We need a suitable symbolic representative outside—an easily recognized authority figure who can fit the part, might discover our wrongdoings and bring retribution on us. What better symbol than the policeman who has a badge, club, gun and wears the uniform of authority—a perfect scapegoat. Quite a neat psychological trick. Now the thing to be avoided is out there. We can run away from it, fight it, restrain it, heap abuse on it, and through it all we can feel guiltless and even self-righteous.

The uncomfortable feelings that were internal before will now be attributed to our feared authority representative—feeling of being observed, the feeling of being detected, the pleasure in getting away with something illicit and above all, the tremendous release from guilt and anxiety now that we no longer have the *policeman-authority* inside of us.

Obviously, problems of conscience are greater for some people than for others. Those who have come to terms with their internal conflicts can partially identify with the aggressor and so feel equal to and able to cope with authority and criticism. Those who have not been unable to resolve this conflict to a significant degree, reveal their distress by way of exaggerated reactions to authority and an intense need to utilize an external symbol as a scapegoat.

In this sense the policeman serves above and beyond the call of duty by making himself available as the scapegoat. He is a highly visible object conflicted people can butt up against and gain distance from in struggling with their unresolved conflicts over dependency, independence, and authority. Other minority groups as well as policemen have always served in this function—"wops, polacks, kikes, niggers, and spics."[21]

Some Typical Reactions—Cynicism and Aloofness

By the very nature of their work, policemen are constantly exposed to the seamy side of life. This can lead to a generally negative view of people and the feeling that everybody is an idiot and nothing is any good. The extremely cynical attitude is often accompanied by depression, anger and a need to maintain distance. A common way of coping with cynicism is by putting up a wall, becoming aloof from people and feeling superior. However, a depressed, angry man is not able to function as effectively as a calm, optimistic one.

The cynical, aloof attitude tends to get communicated to others and exerts an influence on transactions which should be routine, but which become exaggerated with over-reactions occurring. Cynicism is different from skepticism, which is a healthy and necessary attitude in maintaining one's balance. The skeptical attitude is one of alertness, of not taking things for granted, and of reserving judgment until underlying motives are considered.

BIBLIOGRAPHY

1. Aaron, James and Shafter, Albert: *The Police Officer and Alcoholism.* Springfield, Thomas, 1963.
2. *Alcohol and Alcoholism.* National Institute of Mental Health, 1969.
3. *Alcohol, Alcoholism and Law Enforcement.* Law Enforcement Study Center, Washington University, 1969.
4. Bem, Daryl: *Beliefs, Attitudes and Human Affairs.* Belmont, Brooks-Cole, 1970.
5. Black, Hillel: *Buy Now, Pay Later.* Caldwell, Morrow, 1961.
6. Blane, Howard: *The Personality of the Alcoholic.* New York, Harp T., 1968.
7. Bourne, Peter: Military psychiatry and the Viet Nam experience. *American Journal of Psychiatry,* October, 1970, pp. 481-488.
8. Cohen, Bernard: *The Police Internal Administration of Justice in New York City.* New York, Rand, November, 1970.
9. Cohen, Bernard and Chaiken, Jan: *Police Background Characteristics and Performance: Summary.* The New York City Rand Institute, May, 1972.
10. *Conference Leadership Manual for Police Officers.* Los Angeles Police Department, 1969.
11. Danish, Steven and Brodsky, Stanley: Training of policemen in emotional control and awareness. *American Psychologist,* 1970, pp. 368-369.
12. *F.B.I. Law Enforcement Bulletin,* February, 1972.
13. Hollingsworth, Dan: *Rocks in the Roadway.* Hollingsworth, 1971.
14. Hooke, James and Krauss, Herbert: Personality characteristics of successful police sergeant candidates. *The Journal of Criminal Law, Criminology, and Police Science,* Vol. 62, No. 1, pp. 104-106.
15. Levinson, H.: *Executive Stress.* New York, Harp T., 1970.

16. Johnson, Deborah and Gregory, Robert: Police-community relations in the United States: A Review of recent literature and projects. *The Journal of Criminal Law, Criminology, and Police Science,* Vol. 62, No. 1, 1971, pp. 94-103.
17. Neff, Walter: *Work and Human Behavior.* New York, Atherton, 1968.
18. Newman, L. E. and Steinberg, J. L.: Consultation with police on human relations training. *American Journal of Psychiatry,* April, 1970, pp. 65-73.
19. Niederhoffer, Arthur: *Behind the Shield: The Police in Urban Society.* Garden City, Doubleday, 1967.
20. *Police Training and Performance Study.* Law Enforcement Assistance Administration, PR 70-4, September, 1970.
21. Reiser, Martin: A psychologist's view of the badge. *The Police Chief,* September, 1970, pp. 24-26.
22. Runkel, Peter: *The Law Unto Themselves.* Planarian Press, 1970.
23. Sayles, Leonard and Strauss, George: *Human Behavior in Organizations.* Englewood Cliffs, P-H, 1966.
24. Sikes, M. P. and Cleveland, S. E.: Human relations training for police and community. *American Psychologist,* August, 1969, pp. 766-769.
25. Skolnick, Jerome: *Justice Without Trial.* Somerset, Wiley, 1966.
26. Sterling, James: *Changes in Role Concepts of Police Officers During Recruit Training.* International Association of Chiefs of Police, June, 1969.
27. Storr, Anthony: *Human Aggression.* New York, Atheneum, 1968.
28. Talbott, John: Training police in community relations and urban problems. *American Journal of Psychiatry,* January, 1971, pp. 894-900.
29. Wagner, Richard and Sherwood, John (eds.): *The Study of Attitude Change.* Belmont, Brooks-Cole, 1969.
30. Walker, Robert: *Changing Roles of Police Officers.* Mimeo.
31. Walther, Regis: McCune, Shirley and Trojanowicz, Robert: The contrasting cultures of policemen and social workers. Mimeo, 1969.
32. Watson, Nelson: *Improving Officer-Citizen Contacts.* International Association of Chiefs of Police, 1969.
33. Watson, Nelson: *Attitudes—A Factor in Performance.* International Association of Chiefs of Police, 1969.
34. Watson, Nelson: *Issues in Human Relations: Threats and Challenges.* International Association of Chiefs of Police, 1969.
35. Watson, Nelson and Sterling, James: *Police and Their Opinions.* International Association of Chiefs of Police, 1969,

CHAPTER THREE

MARRIAGE, DIVORCE AND FAMILY PROBLEMS

ALTHOUGH MARITAL AND FAMILY problems are not unique to men in police work, the occupational stresses and demands do frequently have an influence on these important relationships. It has been rumored that policemen have the highest divorce rate of any occupational group. However, there does not appear to be any factual data to support this notion.

A recent informal survey reported in the press by the Seattle Police Department indicated that 60 percent of their new officers were divorced within three years on the job. A more recent (1971) survey within the Los Angeles Police Department indicated a 5 percent divorce experience during the first three years of employment and an overall divorce ratio of 21.1 percent.[17]

The latest divorce figures from the National Center for Health Statistics continue to increase at a staggering rate. In 1969 the divorce-marriage ratio for all occupations nationwide was 31.1 percent. The most recent figure for early 1972 is 45.5 percent.[24]

In 1969, the ratio of divorce to marriage in California was 48.8 percent. The latest California ratio is 75.5 percent or three divorces for every four marriages. Yet, California trails Montana (80.3%) and Oregon (76.8%).

A 1969 nationwide sample of policemen found that 93 percent of experienced officers were married and only 3 percent divorced or separated.[25] A later national study in 1971 showed 63.2 percent of policemen married and 5.9 percent divorced or separated.[22]

One can conclude from the above data, that, nationwide, people are divorcing more than ever. Easing of the divorce process and changes in societal values are probably key factors. The figures on policemen populations lag considerably behind the national averages. This suggests some greater stability and a high value on marriage and family. As one study put it:

> Policemen are family men. . . . Moreover, policemen seem to have more stable marriages than are to be found in the community as a whole. . . . Policemen represent family men, men who value family stability highly and who may rely on their families for support against a populace which they often regard as hostile.[3]

ON SELECTING A PARTNER

We operate with two agendas when selecting a partner for a close personal relationship. Consciously we tend to be aware of physical attractiveness, sex appeal, personality traits, mood characteristics, mutual responsiveness and admiration. On the unconscious level we may be looking for something quite different.

If there are strong underlying needs for punishment or being dominated, we may unknowingly look for a partner who is aggressive and critical. If there is underlying insecurity and self-doubt, we may look for a partner who will idealize, adore and give constant reassurance to our shaky self-concept.

Values in our society have been skewed to extremes. On one side is the emphasis on material things and tangibles while on the other is the over-idealized romantic notion of love. This value surfaces in such clichés as *love is blind, love conquers all,* and in the fantasy that love causes bells to ring, and lights to flash.

The perpetuation of this unrealistic notion of love often leads to an inevitable puncturing of the romantic fantasies, to disillusionment and depression. In contrast to the romantic concept of an intimate relationship is the acceptance of reality. This involves an awareness that the fantasy of a one and only true love is a construct rather than a fact.

Actually, there are hundreds of individuals in the world who would make eminently satisfactory life partners. However, because of our own limited areas of mobility and familiarization we usually don't ever get the opportunity to meet and know these potential mates.

In selecting a partner it is important to value inner qualities and to realize that outer facade is of secondary importance. Physical appearances will change and one will age. However, the personal attitudes of optimism, giving, sharing, honesty, openness, and accepting what is real rather than holding out for perfection, are much more important in the long run.

Obviously, it is very difficult to know in depth and in advance what a potential mate's needs and desires are. Needs differ in people and in the same person over time. In this connection, the more one understands himself, the greater the probability of sensitive awareness and understanding of the other person. In many relationships, some early, objective premarital counseling can lead to greater insight and more rational choices.

VALUES IN MARRIAGE

Once the romantic newness has worn off to some degree, other more practical questions arise which have to do with what is important and what each partner values in the marriage relationship.

What Is A Good Marriage?

When you consider that two separate individuals with different life styles and value systems, each used to satisfying his and her own needs, get together in a marriage relationship with minimal preparation, it is amazing that as many marriages last as long as they do.

Contrary to the romantic expectation that marriage should be a continual honeymoon, durable ones are really based on compromises and adjustments.

In a good workable marriage each partner has to *sacrifice* quite a bit. He has to subordinate his own selfish needs and interests to giving. He has to think *we* instead of *I* and *you* in the marriage relationship.

It is very difficult to have a workable marriage unless both partners are fairly adult. Being adult means the ability to see the partner as most important, deserving of love, consideration, and tenderness, and of sacrifice if necessary.

Sharing, Love and Security

Attitudes and value systems about marriage have been changing over the years as have attitudes about other social institutions. In order to work in our society today, marriage should be a form of equal partnership with openness, mutual respect and sharing. Although the husband may still be nominal head of the family, analogous to the chairman of the board of directors, the wife is an equal stockholder and voting member of the board.

Sharing involves the kind of openness in which you really want to understand the other person's feelings and point of view. Self-interest is satisfied best by pleasing the partner. The partner comes first on the totem pole in terms of priorities.

Sharing includes letting each other in on personal feelings, activities, interests, and complaints. This means getting things out on the table, an attitude of leveling with each other honestly in all areas of the relationship. As equal adults, marriage partners are on the same level, looking across at each other rather than looking down or up. Neither is superior, and the dominant atmosphere is one of mutual respect.

Wives of new policemen frequently complain that although they are interested in what happens to their husbands on the job, the husbands often develop the attitude that wives can't possibly understand what a policeman experiences.

In addition, the husband tends to limit his relationships and conversations to other policemen who *understand,* thus unwittingly placing his wife in the position of outsider. When this happens, she begins to feel alone, rejected and unloved.

All too often we still equate love with sexual infatuation and physical attractiveness. Undoubtedly, there are many definitions and kinds of love. However, in the context of a marriage relationship love is a process. It involves a commitment and a desire to understand and to share. It deepens one's own satisfaction by involving a significant other person to help multiply the gratifications one achieves in daily living by giving and sharing.

In this kind of love process there is an acceptance of the real person including shortcomings and imperfections. Time should help deepen the love feelings and increase the satisfactions in a *real* relationship, whereas, if the initial attraction was merely physical and superficial, time will likely result in jaded feelings, boredom, restlessness and a nagging sense of having been cheated.

Love and hate are opposite sides of a coin and coexist in people. It isn't possible for normal people to only love continuously and constantly without feelings of anger, hatred and resentment occurring periodically in marriage relationships. If these feelings are acknowledged and handled openly without denial or suppression, they can actually help deepen and give more meaning to the relationship.

Feeling secure in marriage is related to knowing where we stand. However, insecurity can also emanate from a negative self-concept as well as from a lack of understanding on the part of the marriage partner. A way to check this is to assess our own value.

If our self-worth is questionable, and there is inner doubt and lack of self-acceptance, we will assume that others feel the same about us. This assumption will also include our mate and we then behave as if this were true. Attributing our own doubts to others affects our social behavior and brings on the very kinds of feared but expected reactions that reinforce our original feelings of inferiority.

Although financial problems are sometimes blamed for insecurity, money is usually a secondary motive. Primarily, we all desire to be recognized, loved and considered worthwhile. From our marriage partner we expect uncritical acceptance, love and honesty. If we know where we stand with our mate, and have an equal give-and-take partnership, we tend to feel secure and satisfied in marriage.

Questions of Time, Trust and Equality

Some of the stress involved in the police occupation is related to problems of time and scheduling. Working nights or mornings, overtime, uncertainty about finishing at the end of watch, being called out on tactical alert or unusual occurrences, can all lead to difficulty at home.

If the marriage is based on a partnership arrangement with mutual respect, the husband understands that letting his wife know he will be late for dinner or will be working overtime is merely a courtesy to a valued partner who cares. It is not being henpecked.

Being married and sharing in a partnership doesn't mean a complete giving up of individuality or separate identity. It is legitimate and desirable for each partner to have some outside interests.

A husband's need to go out occasionally with the boys for a beer, fishing or skiing is understandable. Likewise, if a wife wants to go out with the girls to a show, to play cards, or go bowling, this is understandable also since marriage doesn't require giving up all of one's hobbies or interests.

In order for this kind of arrangement to work satisfactorily there has to be a feeling of basic trust in the marriage relationship. If you trust yourself, you tend to trust others.

An overly possessive or suspicious attitude about one's mate doesn't develop if you are basically secure and self-confident. The feeling of trust in a partner is augmented by the knowledge that you have a solid relationship with no need for sabotaging the partnership. This reinforces one's inner security system.

Policemen have told me that they worry about a wife being alone, feeling that she may be criminally attacked or get into an accident, or in some other way be unable to handle herself if he is not present. Obviously, this indicates insecurity and lack of trust.

If a husband views his wife as really adult, competent and capable, rather than as a helpless child, he will trust her to take care of herself in most situations. This includes knowing she will get help if necessary. However, if he sees her as inadequate, he will tend to assume an over-protective, motherly attitude which results in her feeling anger and resentment over being smothered.

Optimal satisfaction in a marriage is based on equal status and consideration. Male superiority, female dominance, a tug-of-war, competition instead of cooperation are all indicators of inequality which frequently lead to dissatisfaction, anger and even dissolution of marriage. Equality means having the conviction that men and women are equal adult human beings, equally worthwhile and equally important even though individual talents and aptitudes may differ.

Sexual Adventures in Marriage

Sexual attitudes and values are in a state of flux in society. From the prudish, Victorian attitudes of sexual repression and taboo, there has been a large swing of the pendulum in the opposite direction, toward sexual freedom, *group grope*, and *let it all hang out*. The effect of these extremes is to compound problems of sexual adjustment in marriage.

Psychologically, there is a tendency to dichotomize women into the good, pure woman on the pedestal who is like mother, and the impure, fallen woman who is like a prostitute. This dualism divides women into good or bad categories and denies the human realities in the middle.

It creates a conflict when one marries a *good* woman who must also provide sexual satisfaction in spite of being *pure*. The tendency to equate adult sexual behavior with dirty, bathroom activities is a carryover from the childhood which inhibits complete gratification.

There are individuals who can only feel sexually stimulated when dating or engaged, but become overly serious and inhibited in the marriage relationship because they perceive marriage as different.

Marriage is pictured involving rocking chairs, deadly seriousness, routine and boredom. Sex is more of a duty rather than fun, pleasure and an expression of love. Marriage should actually afford the two partners maximal sexual expression and satisfaction.

Presumably marriage partners are attracted to each other, admire, like, value each other. This should result in excellent communication in achieving mutual sexual gratification. Tenderness, concern for the partner's desires and feelings, and open discussion about sexual needs and preferences are all very important in a viable marriage relationship.

Because we are creatures of habit, we tend to do the same things in the same old way, over and over. This can lead to sexual boredom. Perfunctorily having intercourse in the same position and following the same ritual can become stultifying. One needs to maintain an attitude of adventure in sex as well as in other areas when married.

Marriage should not be the end of fun and the onset of depression and gloom. It should be adventurous, stimulating, enjoyable and satisfying. Whether this happens or not depends only on the two partners involved. They can make their sexual relationship whatever they want it to be.

In sex, if each has an attitude of openness, that sex is necessary, important and good, there will be greater likelihood that neither partner will feel misunderstood or frustrated and want to look on the other side of the street for greener pastures.

Experts in sex education feel that no form of sexual activity between man and wife is dirty or unnatural. If both partners desire a particular form of sexual activity and it does not harm either one, it is legitimate and *good*.

For individuals who have severe inhibitions about sexual expression and adventurousness, it sometimes helps to have husband and wife share in reading a sensible book on sexual satisfaction in marriage, several of which are listed in the bibliography.[1, 2, 14, 16, 19, 22] If this isn't sufficient, marriage counseling is strongly recommended.

FAMILY PROBLEMS

Having problems is a normal part of life. It is not the presence of problems that is crucial but how one copes with the problems he has. In family situations, because there are many more participants and many more interactions, it is much more difficult to sort things out in handling these multifaceted problems.

Husband and Wife Roles

Both people usually enter the marriage relationship with an idealized image of what their own and their partner's role should encompass. If the husband's ideal-wife role is envisioned as mainly maid, housekeeper, baby-sitter and cook, or if the wife sees the husband's role as primarily that of meal ticket, chances are there will be serious problems.

Admittedly fantasy has an essential function in making life tolerable. However, fantasy should be tempered by reality. The ideal images and role expectations that each partner brings to the marriage almost always include elements from early child-hood family relationships.

The wife is expected to be a composite of mother, teacher, nurse and actress. In all of these parts she is supposed to be per-fect. However, in reality there are no perfect people. Rarely does life closely approximate fantasy, so the ideal expectations are doomed to disappointment and failure. Unless husband and wife are willing to accept the real person with faults and imperfections rather than holding out for the unreal ideal-image with its per-fectionism, unhappiness is inevitable.

Another type of role game-playing which also leads to conflict is where husband is unconsciously equated with father and the wife assumes a little girl role.

As she matures in the marriage relationship, the wife will no longer be satisfied with the helplessness and dependency con-nected with playing the little girl. She will demand more of an adult role, but the husband may resent this since she is no longer the sweet little girl he married.

As each matures and grows in marriage, modification in role expectations are necessary as are more tolerance and understand-ing. Husbands and wives normally occupy a multitude of roles in marriage, but if the expectations are kept pristine and inflex-ible by either partner, it is sure to result in frustration. Each must allow and encourage the other to mature and grow as a person within the marriage partnership.

The Children, Parents and In-Laws

Children are neither chips off the old block nor appendages of their parents. They become separate individuals right at birth when the cord is cut. As such they have uniqueness, individuality and need to become increasingly independent as they develop and utilize their innate capabilities. While young and limited in self-sufficiency and judgment, children need protection and limit-setting consistent with their developing adequacy.

One of the greatest satisfactions a parent should have is the knowledge that the formerly dependent, late teenage child has become a self-sufficient, independent person who is able to stand on his own two feet and make his own decisions. Parents must have assurance and security enough to cut the apron strings rather than remaining dominant, overly protective or wanting to hold on to a dependent child.

Children often serve as scapegoats in the family situation for the frustrations and resentments of parents. We tend to see in the child our own hated faults and to punish for them severely.

We also set very high expectations for children, often higher than they are capable of attaining at their developmental level. We may expect them to be little adults when, in reality, they are little children. Childhood is a time of fun, of exploration, of curiosity and learning. It is not the time for over-seriousness or impossible demands and standards.

Expectations and suggestions have power. If we have negative expectations of a child, we unconsciously help shape the very behavior we dislike and disapprove of. The result is a self-fulfilling prophecy. When mother predicts that little Jimmy is bad and will wind up in jail just like Uncle George, frequently with anger and rejection, those suggestions and expectations will be internalized and influence little Jimmy.

Unconsciously, Jimmy feels he is doing what mother expects him to and thus is satisfying her. At the same time he is also punishing her for rejecting and treating him negatively. Discipline is much more effective when it is positive and sets a constructive example.

Getting married and establishing a family successfully requires a modicum of autonomy and freedom of choice. This includes independence of and equality with one's own parents as well as the in-laws.

Marriage partners must rate first with each other. Children, parents, in-laws, and friends come second if there is to be a viable marriage. Married people who tolerate interference from parents or in-laws or who are overly dependent on them are inviting disharmony and anger.

Those parents who still view their married offspring as *my little boy* or *my little girl* have a problem of letting go. If the offspring go along with this pretense, it becomes a game which they are sharing in and perpetuating. Parents and offspring have to be aware and acknowledge they are now equal adults, with opinions, attitudes and values having equal validity and weight.

Some Games Spouses Play

Eisenstein[9] has discussed neurotic interaction in marriage, Berne[4, 5] has described some of the games that people play, and Lederer and Jackson[13] have outlined some of the common myths and fallacies of marriage. Policemen and wives, being human, may also be playing games with each other without consciously being aware of it and without having much fun as a result.

Most of the games that policemen and wives play are based on unconscious needs and desires which originate during childhood, but are carried over and get re-enacted in the marriage relationship. A good clue that one of these games is being played is the repetitious nature of the conflict. This has been labeled *the broken record* syndrome.[18]

Some of the games are based on the fallacy that women are inferior to men, particularly sexually. This is a myth that has been perpetuated for decades. In many ways women can outperform men. This includes sexual performance. Aside from muscular strength, women as a group have greater adaptability and durability. This is shown ultimately in the actuarial statistics comparing male and female birth rates and longevity.[11]

A fairly common game that policemen and wives may play is that of husband as superwife. In this game the husband as inspecting officer is hypercritical and keeps his wife intimidated in an inferior position by showing her that he is a better wife than she.

He does this by invading those areas traditionally reserved for the woman which reflect female capability. Whether cooking, housecleaning or taking care of the kids, the husband belittles, then runs rings around his wife while he lets her know it in many direct and indirect ways.

The new wife may go along with this game for a period of time, but as she matures she frequently gets tired of it, grows frustrated, angry and begins to assert her independence and individuality. At this point the conflict surfaces in full bloom.

Another typical game is one in which wife is cast as mother, or husband plays father, or both. Setting up the marriage partner in this parental role prevents an equal adult relationship from developing. It also provides a channel for childhood fears, resentments, unrealistic expectations and fantasies to be reactivated in the context of the marriage situation.

There will likely be sexual difficulties and conflicts around the unresolved dependency. After all, how can one have a satisfactory sexual relationship with one's parent when incest is taboo in our society?

Still another game involves the husband as dictator and Don Juan and wife as frigid and sexually inadequate little girl. In this game the husband attempts to maintain his uncertain male adequacy by ruling with an iron fist and proving his sexual prowess by having intercourse with as many females as possible. It also bolsters his ego to see his wife as frigid, sexually inadequate and lacking in know-how compared to the *street-type* women he seems to prefer.

The wife on her part may subtly encourage her husband to continue the game by setting up a cat and mouse arrangement wherein they alternate roles and tote up who is getting away with what. Variations on the cat and mouse arrangement could be labeled cops and robbers, or the hurter and the hurtee.

A sidelight to this game is that couples find it difficult to spend much time alone together. They either attend parties or arrange to always have other people present to reduce the extreme anxiety and discomfort they feel at the prospect of real intimacy. This game also requires the inducing of guilt in one partner and the inflicting of pain on the other one.

A common situation that policemen may get into is the job-above-family-and-wife, and children-as-suspects game. In this game, children and wife are classed with suspects who can be interrogated using third degree methods. Feeling extreme distrust and jealousy, the husband feels self-righteous and justified in placing his job above everything else. His wife's needs and complaints are rationalized as a lack of understanding and competition with his job.

The *I am going to reform you* game involves the educational or intellectual superiority of one of the partners and the need to make a better person out of the inferior one.

If the wife has a bachelor's or graduate degree and the husband is only a high school graduate, the wife may see her mission in life as pushing and improving her husband so that he will become as worthwhile and acceptable as she is.

The husband plays the game by feeling intellectually inferior and therefore distant and uncomfortable with his wife. The wife can feel superior as she views her husband as a narrow-minded clod who can't possibly understand literature, philosophy, or humanistic problems.

For any of these games to be initiated and continue, it takes two players. If one of the partners refuses to play and disengages from the game, it can't continue. Sometimes professional counseling is necessary in order to have the people become aware that a game is being played, the type of game, and then deal with the unconscious gratification derived from it.

There are an endless number of games that can be labeled. However, they all have in common the fact that they stem from early conflicts and motives outside of one's awareness and have the repetitious quality of a broken record.

Common Symptoms of Family Distress

Symptoms are often indicators of underlying problems and do not necessarily constitute the problem itself. Infidelity, drinking excessively, gambling, obesity, poor communications and sexual incompatibility are all common symptoms of marital or family distress.

Because communication is essential in interpersonal relationships, it functions as a kind of barometer of the emotional climate in the family. With an attitude of understanding, closeness, positive concern and respect, communication can be open and nonthreatening. With emotional distancing and defensiveness, walls are erected which make communication difficult if not impossible.

One of the emotional tragedies in our society results from the concept of manliness as requiring coolness, lack of expression of emotion and acting like the rock of Gibraltar.

We teach children that strong men are not supposed to cry or become emotionally upset. This lays the groundwork for later communication difficulties in marital and family situations because communication requires the expression of feelings as well as attitudes and ideas. But if feelings are supposed to be kept tightly controlled, then communication must be constrained.

In a good husband-wife relationship, it is absolutely essential for openness, honesty and directness in communicating needs and feelings. False modesty, pride and mistaken notions about what constitutes manliness can cause more harm than all of the financial difficulties combined. This can be a serious problem for the husband who has to learn that feelings are legitimate, that tenderness and expressions of love are necessary and desirable in a marriage relationship.

For many men, it is easy to express critical, angry and negative feelings, but positive, tender, affectionate feelings are communicated with great difficulty.

If we care about someone enough to marry and want to spend a significant part of our lives with that person, we should want to be open and honest about all of our feelings with that individual.

Sexual incompatibility or conflicts are frequent symptoms of marital distress. The sexual relationship between two people is a function of emotional closeness. With mutual respect, understanding, and concern, there is usually good sexual communication. Poor sexual communication results from emotional distance, coldness, lack of understanding and a primary interest in selfish gratification.

Infidelity, gambling, heavy drinking and emphasis on material things rather than on feelings can also be escape hatches and attempts to reduce anxiety and tension. With a good marriage relationship, the routine sexual temptations which surround us constantly are in themselves not enough to sway our behavior. However, if we are dissatisfied, unhappy, angry and resentful, we will find many reasons to allow ourselves to be tempted into acting-out.

The taking of sides is another symptom of family distress. Wife and children can put themselves on one side of the fence and push the husband to the other side. A clue to this symptom is the wife's talking about *the children and me* without separating out how she feels. She allies herself with the children as a sibling.

What she is communicating is a feeling of rejection and the

need for support. In her unhappiness she uses the children for gratification. A clue to this type of distress in the family is the use of the pronouns *you* and *me* rather than *we* and *our*.

The Middle-Age Syndrome

Middle-age has some predictable problems built into it. If we are forewarned, we can be better prepared to cope with them. For both men and women middle-age is a summing up, evaluating time of life. It is also a distinct developmental stage of transition in terms of physiological and psychological functioning.

The middle-age man assesses himself to see if he has achieved the goals he set for himself when younger. He also has to accept the fact that he has slowed down physically, can't run as fast, hit as hard, and can no longer maintain the self-image of a young athlete. He has to change his self-concept.

In a similar fashion the wife takes stock of herself physically and in terms of accomplishments. Feelings of depression are common during this time of life because of hormone changes and because of guilt over lack of achievement. There is the recognition of growing old and transient feelings of hopelessness and wondering where life has gone.

These feelings can lead to insecurity and a pulling apart of the marriage relationship if either partner looks for reassurance outside in extramarital affairs or compulsive work activities. However, it can also lead to a frank personal reassessment and feelings of self-acceptance and a renewed more meaningful marriage relationship.

If one is successful in updating his self-image, he can accept his new middle-age status without a sense of loss and inadequacy. He feels a sense of achievement and knows that the future still lies ahead with much more to be accomplished. Middle-age should be a period of growth and satisfaction rather than a time of anxiety, worry, and self-doubt.[10]

SEPARATION AND DIVORCE

Not all marriages are made in heaven and not all people can live happily ever after in marriage. For some, the act of separation or divorce may be an indication of emotional maturity and constructive action. However, for too many others, separation and divorce are indicators of confusion, frustration, anger, dissatisfaction, disillusionment and emotional immaturity. One of the most common symptoms leading to separation and divorce is poor communication.

A Failure to Communicate

The ability to communicate adequately is based on two essential underpinnings. One is a sense of self-worth and the other is a liking and respect for other people. Inner security stems partly from self-acceptance, and the feeling of self-confidence. This required the acceptance of all aspects of yourself, the intellectual, the physical, the sexual, the soft, the hard and the unreasonable.

With self-acceptance, a person can reveal himself without feeling threatened. He can show various facets of his personality, value system, attitudes and feelings without fearing criticism and without generating self-guilt. For the married man in police work, this means accepting his warm, tender, love feelings as well as the hard, intellectual, logical thoughts.

One of the barriers to understanding is an overly critical attitude based on perfectionistic tendencies. If a wife is expected to be perfect, she can never measure up and the marriage won't provide complete satisfaction.

If there is an emphasis on material things rather than on human values, the marriage relationship can degenerate into occasional excitement over an increasing bank account or acquisition of a piece of property. The deeper satisfaction of being close, of sharing feelings and of desiring to satisfy each other's needs improves communication verbally and nonverbally.

Sometimes a trial separation is useful in bringing out in a forceful way, the mutual needs and feelings that have been taken for granted by one partner or the other. Out of this realization can come a clearer awareness and understanding of the meaning of closeness and communication. Unfortunately, all too often separations represent a kind of yo-yo game with bouncing back and forth going on endlessly. Remorse gives way to resentment and vice versa as the partners move back together and then away from each other.

One of the forgotten essentials in good communication is the art of listening. Real listening involves focusing completely on what the other person is saying whether you agree with it or not.

If husband and wife talk at, instead of with, each other, are defensive, struggling for power using words as daggers or clubs, there will be a tug-of-war rather than two-way communication. Defensiveness increases distortion and misinterpretation of the message. If we are secure and at ease with ourselves, we can afford to listen more carefully and not have to guard our own viewpoint as zealously.

Lederer and Jackson[13] give some interesting exercises that husbands and wives can use in attempting to improve communication, and Bach[1] describes some techniques for fighting fair in a marriage relationship which can improve communications and understanding.

Status, Power and Immaturity

One of the common questions that comes up in a counseling situation with husbands and wives who have been having marital problems is *Who wears the pants in the family?* Basically, this relates to competitive strivings with each marital partner desiring to be in the top position. Who is in charge, who has the status, and who is superior seem to be the questions.

The partner who feels he has the status in the marriage may not necessarily have the power. Frequently, quiet and passive people are content to be the power behind the throne without necessarily needing open recognition and status.

In the past many women would rationalize their *inferior* role as wife in a marriage situation by feeling that they were responsible for their husband's success and could therefore vicariously share in it. The feeling of power helped to balance her lack of status in the marriage situation. However, both status and power involve a need for recognition and importance.

In an equal partnership marriage these needs are satisfied by mutual respect and sharing. Each partner openly acknowledges the essential qualities and equal importance of the other. Instead of a tug-of-war each feels on the same team, working for the same goals.

Immaturity is a term used to describe an individual who retains many of his childlike behaviors when they should have been given up. These include selfishness rather than a strong sense-of-self, the inability to share equally, the need to maintain self-esteem by feeling superior, and looking down on other people, including the spouse, as inferiors. Long held immaturities which result from inappropriate influences carried over from the past may require professional counseling assistance in order to bring them into awareness and then have them relegated to the scrap heap.

BIBLIOGRAPHY

1. Bach, George: *The Intimate Enemy.* New York, Avon, 1968.
2. Baruch, Dorothy and Miller, Hyman: *Sex in Marriage.* New York: Harp T., 1962.
3. Bayley, David H.: *Minorities and the Police.* New York, The Free Pr, 1966.
4. Berne, Eric: *Games People Play.* New York, Grove, 1964.
5. Berne, Eric: *What Do You Say After You Say Hello?* New York, Grove, 1972.
6. Brodey, Warren: *Changing the Family.* New York, Potter, 1968.
7. Carter, Hugh and Glick, Paul: *Marriage and Divorce: A Social and Economic Study.* Cambridge, Harvard U Pr, 1970.
8. Cooley, Leland: *The Retirement Trap.* Garden City, Doubleday, 1965.
9. Eisenstein, Victor: *Neurotic Interaction in Marriage.* New York, Basic, 1956.
10. *Generation in the Middle.* Blue Cross of Southern California, 1970.
11. Hunt, Morton: *The World of the Formerly Married.* New York, McGraw, 1966.
12. Kasirsky, Gilbert: *Vasectomy, Manhood and Sex.* New York, Springer Pub, 1972.
13. Lederer, William and Jackson, Don: *The Mirages of Marriage.* New York, Norton, 1968.
14. O'Neill, Nena and George: *Open Marriage.* New York, Evans, 1972.
15. Popenoe, Paul: *Preparing for Marriage.* Los Angeles, The American Institute of Family Relations #1, 1968.
16. Rainer, Jerome and Maria: *Sexual Adventure in Marriage.* New York, S & S, 1965.
17. Reiser, Martin and Saxe, Susan: *Divorce Experience in an Urban Police Department.* Presented at the California State Psychological Association Convention, Los Angeles, January 29, 1972.

18. Reiser, Martin: The psychologist's corner. *Beat Magazine,* January, 1973.
19. Reuben, David: *Everything You Always Wanted to Know About Sex.* New York, McKay, 1970.
20. Rogers, Carl R.: *Becoming Partners: Marriage and its Alternatives.*
21. Steinzor, Bernard: *When Parents Divorce.* New York, Pantheon, 1969.
22. Sterling, James: *Changes in the Role Concepts of Police Officers.* International Association of Chiefs of Police, 1972.
23. Van De Velde, Theodor H.: *Ideal Marriage.* New York, Random, 1965.
24. *Vital and Health Statistics.* National Center for Health Statistics, Washington, D.C., 1972.
25. Watson, Nelson and Sterling, James: *Police and their Opinions.* International Association of Chiefs of Police, 1969.

CHAPTER FOUR

EMOTIONAL DEVELOPMENT AND MENTAL HEALTH

POLICE OFFICERS DEAL with mental health problems on the job every day. The professional policeman knows that in addition to the problems of citizens and suspects his own inner security and emotional state profoundly influence the outcome of routine transactions. Increasingly, the modern officer is not only interested in how to handle the emotionally disturbed person, but also in the dynamics of the problem. These are legitimate and necessary knowledge areas in deepening his evolving professionalism.

INFLUENCES ON PERSONALITY DEVELOPMENT

Although there are influences throughout life which affect personality development, the process can be viewed as analogous to a pyramid structure. The wide base of the pyramid represents the earliest years of life and forms the basic foundation for emotional stability.

There is considerable evidence that as early as age six or seven much of one's permanent personality structure has been built.[9] The structure is added to, modified and sometimes renovated after the early years, but the basic architecture remains.

Inner Drives, Values, Self, Conscience and Value System

Human beings have survival motives, social motives and ego-integrative motives. Survival motives or drives are related to bodily needs such as hunger, thirst and fear. Social motives include drives such as maternal, sex, dominance and submission, and aggression. Ego-integrative motives include a drive for achievement, sometimes called achievement-motivation and other goal-directed behavior. An important fact is that motives are not only conscious but also unconsciously based.

Unconscious motivation sometimes leads to irrational or unusual behavior. Drives such as manipulation, activity, and curiosity are not directly related to physiological bases, but still seem to be important needs in human beings. Those drives which emanate from within the individual not only insure his survival, but also the development of more complex behavior. The self-integrative drives are essential to the development of one's self-concept which results in a personal identity and the ability to differentiate oneself from other organisms.

Conscience is a mix of internalized limits and restrictions residing in the individual. As these become elaborated and are juxtaposed against ego-integrative drives, a value system emerges whose function is to allow the individual to live with minimal internal and environmental conflict.

Outer—Important Adults, Wider Environment

A person exists and grows in a particular environment. Many significant environmental influences impinge on and help to shape some of the internal structure. Parents and other important adults in the child's environment are crucial in this regard. As models for the child they gratify survival needs, set standards and limits and also supply the basic learning which the child emulates and internalizes as part of his developing personality structure.

Parents represent the world and ensure physical and emotional survival to the child. As the child develops, becomes less dependent on parents and exercises his new social skills, he can move away from the home situation and begin to explore and learn from the wider environment. But he can do this only after he has established a sense of confidence and adequacy based on what he has learned earlier in his own family situation.

Interesting work by Spitz[20] has indicated convincingly that the first year of life is critical. What follows is based on the many important emotional events occurring in the infant's early life. In extreme cases, it can become a life and death question based on the amount and quality of emotional gratification of basic affectual needs of the infant. Without adequate *mothering*, arrested development or even death may occur.

Physical Factors—Hormones, Diet and Exercise

Hormone imbalance caused by physiological malfunction, diet, or trauma can result in physical and psychological dysfunction. The proper balance of male and female sex hormones appears to be necessary if the individual is to develop adequately.

In cases of hormone imbalance or malfunction, it is possible to supplement or balance body chemistry by prescribed medication. This is commonly done to counter hormone deficiency when testicles or ovaries are removed, and for menopausal conditions resulting from diminished female hormone output.

Both sexes seem to have cycles over the month. Periods of high energy and well-being may alternate with apathy and indifference. However, the critical factor seems to be basic life style rather than the fluctuations in it.

Diet has come under increasing scrutiny lately in terms of its role in maintaining physical and emotional health. Not only amounts of food, but kinds of food seem to be significant in maintaining equilibrium.

Nutritionists today[22] feel that refined sugar is a culprit which leads to tooth decay, to excess weight and cardiovascular problems. Protein foods on the other hand provide long-range energy and the necessary building blocks for maintenance of life.

Increasingly, the trio of smoking, sugar, and coffee are being looked upon as harmful and disruptive of healthy functioning.

Overweight is a common problem in our society and is frequently related to emotional frustration with overeating as a compensatory mechanism. There are many fads and forms of diet propounded and many of them will work on a short-term basis. However, the reality is that for long-range success, diet is not effective without a change in one's eating habits. This means accepting the nutritional importance of protein foods and minimizing sugar and starches, the carbohydrate group.

In addition to eating patterns, maintaining a desired weight is related to one's self-concept and sense of worth. If a person feels worthwhile and deserving of looking attractive, he is willing to do what is required to achieve that goal. However, if he unconsciously feels unworthy, guilty or unacceptable, in spite of conscientious dieting and daily weighing, his long-range goal will probably be frustrated because of his unconscious need for self-criticism and punishment.

The lack of exercise may well kill us in the long run. As members of the animal kingdom we were provided with muscles which must be exercised in order to remain healthy. However, our way of life in Western society with its technology, urbanization and emphasis on leisure and non-exertion have led to serious muscular disuse and consequent development of a variety of psycho-physical symptoms.

There is some evidence to suggest[12, 16] that adequate exercise can have beneficial effects on a wide range of psychosomatic disturbances. These include such ailments as migraine headaches, ulcers, backaches, colitis, asthma, arthritis, skin conditions and hypertension.

Some interesting research recently[1] has shown that we tend to operate on the basis of a circadian rhythm. This means that man and other animals are affected by day and night, and biologically adapt by devloping certain cycles or rhythms. One of the interesting findings was that male sex hormone production seems to be at its maximum early in the morning rather than late at night, although we are accustomed to thinking of nighttime for sexual activity.

Diet and exercise appear to be closely related to the problem of heart attacks in our society.[18] More and more men and women are being affected earlier in life by disabling cardiovascular disturbances. One of the culprits in the development of atherosclerosis or fatty deposits on the walls of the arteries, is cholesterol.

Although cholesterol is a necessary substance manufactured by the body, its concentration in the blood can also be increased by diet, stress, and lack of exercise. In addition to cholesterol, fatty substances called triglycerides seem to be involved. Although excessive amounts of cholesterol in the blood correlate positively with probability of coronaries, when cholesterol and triglycerides are both high, the likelihood increases significantly.

One prediction table indicates that at age forty with increased cholesterol and triglycerides the probability of a coronary is 75 percent and at age fifty-five there is a 91 percent chance of an attack. A simple test called phenotyping can determine whether the rise in these substances is caused by diet, physiological dysfunction, or genetic inheritance. In many cases, proper diet, exercise and perhaps medication can halt or reverse this process.

MENTAL HEALTH—WHAT IS NORMAL?

The term *normal* has been misunderstood over the years. It isn't simply the presence or absence of something. Normality is hard to describe because it is a statistical concept which is based on the rule of the majority. What most people are like in a society constitutes the norm. This varies in different subcultures.

The Continuum of Mental Health

Although it is easier and appears to save energy to put labels on people, and to view mental health as being either absent or present, emotional or mental health is actually a range or continuum of behaviors. In the center of the mental health continuum is normality which represents the majority of people with a wide range of individual traits and idiosyncrasies.

Rather than asking if someone is normal, the essential question is, can the person cope adequately in his daily life? How well-adjusted is he inwardly and in his interpersonal relationships in the environment? All people have problems of one kind or another. The issue is not the presence of problems but how the problems are coped with that determines one's mental health.

At the extreme low end of the mental health continuum are severe disturbances in internal and environmental coping reflected in poor reality-testing, an inability for adequate self-care, or being a danger to self or to someone else. The gravely disabled individual may be labeled psychotic or borderline psychotic, or with somewhat better coping, a neurotic.

At the upper end of the emotional health continuum are those individuals who are extremely emotional stable, who have had just the right combination of factors in their early environment genetically and developmentally to predispose them to handling stress in an optimal way with minimum interference in their everyday functioning. This group has been studied very little.

It is important to conceptualize mental health not as a static state, but as a fluid process. A person's functioning level varies on a day-to-day, weekly or monthly basis, particularly under stress situations. It is possible for any individual, no matter how stable, to crack mentally under certain circumstances with sufficient stress and tension being applied.

However, most of us establish an equilibrium and stabilize our functioning, so that we operate within a particular range of the mental health continuum. Unless some unusual trauma or stress situation devlops to temporarily displace us from our accustomed adjustment, we usually maintain our established coping pattern.

Love and Hate, Conscience and Reality

The main forces which tend to influence our emotional state and behavior are love and hate, our inner sense of right and wrong, and our striving for mastery over the environment. Love and hate are strong forces that operate at both conscious and unconscious levels.

It is common to love and hate someone simultaneously or have one side of the ambivalence predominating. In extreme situations the love-hate conflict may be so severe that *killing with kindness* may emerge as a symptom.

Theoretically, warmth, tenderness and affection derive from the constructive drives which include the self-preservative needs. Hate emanates from the destructive drives which relate to rage, self-punishment or death. Ideally the constructive and destructive drives are fused and help to control and channel each other. This allows some of the energy from both drives to be used to the individual's advantage.

The content and equality of one's conscience is largely learned. Infants and small children require outside limit setting, guidance and protection because they are not able to provide it for themselves. As they grow, they model themselves after significant admired or feared people in the environment. They internalize some of the personal traits, taboos, prohibitions and values and incorporate them into a personal conscience.

If the environmental influences have been positive, the values and rules of society will be adopted and adhered to by the individual and he will feel guilt if he transgresses these limits. He will also be more self-directed and will value other people's rights as much as he does his own. He operates by his own inner control system.

The individual who has had poor models in the environment may internalize few controls and is less likely to generate guilt to prohibit him from behavior that is detrimental to himself or others. This type of individual remains more outer-directed and like the child will expect someone to stop him from behaving in an undesirable way, to provide external limits since he doesn't have enough inner control or self-motivation.

Small children are curious and need to explore the environment to learn about their surroundings, to master and eventually control their environment. This need for mastery continues as a drive in people throughout life. When the drive for mastery has been positively reinforced, the individual develops a sense of adventurousness, optimism and looking forward to challenges in order to gain satisfaction from exercising his ability to master new situations.

However, if he has been traumatized in the past by being punished or discouraged from exploring, he will probably develop fears and anxieties about new situations and the unfamiliar. This will inhibit and shackle him in later life.

Insecurity coupled with the drive for mastery can lead to a dilemma, the desire for certainty in all things. In this individual, ambiguity or uncertainty causes tension and anxiety and is felt to be intolerable. He may then try to prevent anxiety by using absolutes. He must see things concretely as good or bad rather than exploring further to seek more accurate answers. The ability to tolerate uncertainty and ambiguity is one measure of a person's self-assurance and maturity. This is open-mindedness.

Because much of what we are is learned, we are all very dependent on our unique environment for what we eventually become. The environment includes significant parents and parent substitutes with their ability to provide optimal amounts of love and discipline, and additional influences such as total family situation, school, diet, friends, interpersonal relationships, and value systems. All of these influences interact in various ways to contribute to personality, character structure, and lifestyle.

Some Healthy Qualities

Although mental or emotional health is very difficult to define and is often characterized by an absence of illness, there are some traits related to a healthy state of functioning:

A. A wide variety of sources of gratification.

This involves a variety of interests, ways of satisfying basic needs rather than having all eggs in one basket. It suggests a broad dimension, being well-rounded rather than narrow in regard to sources of satisfaction in life.

B. Flexibility under stress.

Stresses are inherent in living and vary from situation to situation and from month to month. How stresses are handled is the important measure of our emotional stability. If every small and stressful event is perceived and reacted to as a major crisis, then we are constricted and self-limiting. If we can continue to cope flexibly under stress, we retain our perspective and judgment resulting in more constructive options open for handling the stress situations.

C. Recognizing and accepting our own limitations and assets.

We tend to be our own worst enemies. Although most of us have tremendous potential, we utilize only a small portion of it. We tend to limit our own functioning and downgrade our assets. False humility or modesty is a self-limiting attitude with grandiosity as an opposite side of the same coin. By being able to accept our own worth-whileness and value as a human being, we can come to recognize our potentials and aptitudes more realistically and have less need to live in fantasy, feel frustrated and angry.

D. Treating other people as individuals.

If we value ourselves, we also value other people. If we accept ourselves, we accept others. Putting people into pigeonholes and labeling them is convenient, but a highly inaccurate and unfair process. Others must be seen and evaluated as individuals rather than stereotyped.

E. Being active and productive.

All of the genius and potential in the world means very little when it is not used constructively. Extremely high I.Q. is not genius if it is not implemented. In order to achieve we must put into practice our philosophy and our values. When we live what we believe, a sense of well-being and satisfaction results.

STRESS, ANXIETY AND DEFENSES

Stresses are ever present in life, both from internal and external sources. Anxiety is an alerting mechanism and also a measure of our ability to handle tension in a particular stress situation.

Because of the constant bombardment of stimuli from our internal and external environment, we need defenses to protect us from being overwhelmed. The kind and amount of defenses that we utilize are important in successful coping and vary according to personality and how much stress we are attempting to deal with.

Adapting to Stress—The Vital Balance

One measure of emotional health is how we adapt to stress. Typically we try to maintain a balance among inner and outer forces which allows us to function in a state of equilibrium. In this state we are able to cope with the usual kinds of stresses on a day-to-day basis without becoming emotionally upset or unbalanced. Menninger calls this the *vital balance*.[13]

Selye[19] has described what he calls the *general adaptation syndrome* which outlines the general bodily responses to stress. First, an alarm reaction occurs, with some shock, and consequent reduction in activities of the individual, which is followed by a large mobilization of forces to meet the threat. In the second stage, there is a state of resistance to the stress and this state is maintained if the adaptation to the threat is adequate at this level. Third, is the stage of exhaustion where the previously acquired adaptation is lost and the person is no longer able to cope.

Cannon[14] has described homeostasis as a state of equilibrium between subsystems in any organism. This balance protects the body and allows the individual to function without the need to constantly attend and expend energy on the subsystems while external work is being accomplished.

Under an excessive amount of stress, the individual will go into a state of crisis.[10] The previous balance is upset, he feels confused, anxious, overwhelmed and temporarily unable to cope. At this point he can go either way, in a downward spiral emotionally, or he can reconstitute, rearrange his focus and establish an even better emotional adjustment than before. In this regard, a crisis state can have positive value.

Anxiety—Real, Neurotic, and Anticipatory

Anxiety can serve a useful self-preservation function or it can also become an inhibiting interference. Real anxiety is a result of real danger. In this context it is hard to separate fear from the real anxiety someone experiences when facing an attacking animal.

Anxiety can also be lifesaving in alerting us to a potentially dangerous situation and permitting us to take the necessary steps to avoid injury. This anticipatory anxiety stimulates adrenalin flow and the arousal network to put us at the maximum level of efficiency. However, this type of signal anxiety can develop into a problem when felt in a situation which does not justify the signal.

This happens when we react with extreme fear to situations that realistically do not present real danger. Phobias, which are exaggerated learned fears are examples of this. Neurotic anxiety tends to be uncontrolled and usually emanates from fears and unconscious conflicts within the person.

Symptoms—Problems in Coping

When the emotional balance has been upset by excessive stress, our normal defenses are breached and we are no longer able to cope adequately, we develop symptoms or signs of emotional disturbance. Symptoms are not primary causes, but indicators of distress. The individual may develop psychosomatic symptoms such as headache, backache, stomach-ache, diarrhea, ulcers, depression, feelings of being persecuted and in extreme cases, hallucinations and delusions.

Symptoms are idiosyncratic. Why a person develops specific symptoms is difficult to answer. It is likely that there are certain predispositions within organ systems of the individual as well as learned ways of reacting based on models in the early environment and on past successful defensive maneuvers. Although overdetermined, symptoms are useful indicators of the kind of distress and can be interpreted by a trained person. The symptom is a symbolic condensation of the basic underlying conflict, including the wish, the fear and the self-punishment.

Defenses—Normal and Exaggerated

All human beings normally employ a variety of defenses in coping with the ordinary stresses and problems of everyday life. However, if under high stress, our normal defenses are unable to cope with the situation, we will call in additional defenses or intensify those already in operation.

Some of the more common defenses are suppression, repression, displacement, projection, rationalization, reaction-formation, denial, and turning-on-the-self.

These defenses are activated and maintained on an unconscious level. However, it is possible for a person to become aware of his defenses. Suppression is the control of certain impulses and emotions. It may involve keeping in angry or sexual feelings habitually or in situations where they are deemed inappropriate.

Repression is the unconscious forgetting and keeping out of awareness ideas or emotions which are too difficult to handle or are unacceptable. Displacement is the controlling of emotion toward one person and expressing it toward a substitute person or thing. An example of this would be feeling angry at the boss and going home and kicking the dog or yelling at the wife.

Projection is a defense which attempts to get rid of unacceptable feelings by externalizing them onto somebody else in the environment and then attributing the ideas or the feelings to the other person. An extreme example of projection is that of feeling anger and hate toward someone, but because the emotions are unacceptable, they are attributed to the person that one is angry with. The defense becomes, "He is angry at me, and wants to do me in. Therefore, I am justified in feeling some animosity toward him."

Rationalization is the process of making excuses for what we want to do to alleviate our guilt feelings about doing them. For example, a man who gets involved in an extramarital affair may rationalize it by saying all his friends are doing it, so why shouldn't he.

Reaction-formation is the turning of a feeling into its opposite. An example is the milquetoast person who behaves in a very subdued, passive and mild way rather than show his underlying anger and hostility which would make him feel guilty and unworthy. The person who is overly polite and saccharine is also using a reaction-formation defense.

Denial is a defense in which one refuses to accept the reality of a situation. An example is the husband who denies that his wife really means it when she says she wants to divorce him. He is unable to cope with this truth, so he will either not hear what she is saying or interpret it as he wants in order to maintain his equilibrium.

Compensation is another interesting defense because it can be used in a constructive way. The use of this defense helps to make up for shortcomings by developing compensating skills in other areas. An example of this is the boy who has seriously injured his legs and is told he will never walk again. He compensates by rigorous daily exercising and becomes an Olympic runner.

Defenses are useful and necessary in order to help us maintain our emotional equilibrium. However, when they are overused constantly, without an adequate readjustment in emotional balance, our mental economy is strained and chances of emotional upset increase. However, it is important to realize that people generally do the best they are capable of at that point in time.

EMOTIONAL UPSET

Under sufficient stress even the most stable individual will become emotionally upset, and in extreme prolonged situations even mentally ill.

Types of Disorders

There are four main categories of emotional disorders. The first group are the psychoneuroses, or neuroses, which are unsuccessful attempts to handle anxiety. Second, the personality disorders which attempt to displace conflicts toward the outside world and then act-out in a repetitive pattern of behavior.

Third, the psychosomatic disorders which are bodily ailments resulting from the attempt to drain off emotional tension into physical channels. The fourth category includes the psychotic level disorders in which there is ego fragmentation and a significant loss of ability to face reality.

The psychoneuroses are classified according to the nature of the defenses against anxiety.[3]

A. Anxiety Reaction—chronic, diffuse anxiety, palpitations, sweating, nausea, breathing difficulties, diarrhea, indigestion, headaches.

B. Conversion Reaction—inner conflict represented by symbolic somatic disturbances. Hysterical blindness or leg paralysis.

C. Dissociative Reaction—avoids anxiety by walling off consciousness. Amnesia, state of confusion, sleepwalking, multiple personality.

D. Phobic Reaction—one or more severe unrealistic fears such as of animals, dirt, enclosed spaces, heights, water, etc.

E. Obsessive-Compulsive Reaction—persistent unpleasant thoughts (obsessions) and strong impulses to perform repeated ritualistic acts (compulsions). Uses defenses of reaction-formation and undoing.

F. Depressive Reaction—chronic dejection and self-depreciation. Complains and withdraws from social activities.

Personality disorders are known as Character Disorders.

A. Personality Pattern Disturbances—deep-seated problems of personality.

    1. Inadequate Personality—responses to the world are below par—dull.

2. Schizoid Personality—cold, aloof, daydreams and fantasies without any real emotional relationships.
3. Cyclothymic Personality—wide mood swings from elation to severe depression.
4. Paranoid Personality—overly sensitive and suspicious of everyone's motives—complains loudly that world is against him. *Nobody pushes me around.*

B. Personality Trait Disturbances.
   1. Emotionally Unstable Personality—low frustration, tolerance, self-centered and childish.
   2. Passive-Aggressive Personality—may be passive-dependent with clinging and parasitic orientation, or passive-aggressive using passive resistance as in being stubborn or obstinate or aggressive with open hostility and rebelliousness such as in temper tantrums.

C. Sociopathic Personality Disturbances (Psychopathic)—lack of conformity to society's rules and regulations.
   1. Anti-social Reaction—self-centered and pleasure oriented, lacks guilt and doesn't learn from experience—lies, steals, and cheats.
   2. Dyssocial Reactions—relatively mature and stable but comes from environment with distorted values and is in conflict with the law.
   3. Sexual Deviation—sexual immaturity including homosexuality, transvestism, exhibitionism, voyeurism, sadism and masochism.
   4. Addictions—alcohol and drugs.

D. Transient Situational Personality Disorders—acute responses to stress in normal individuals.
   1. Gross Stress Reaction—combat fatigues.
   2. Adult Situation Reaction—react to new situations such as marriage, school, new job, as traumatic.

Psychosomatic Disorders can be categorized as follows:

A. Skin Reactions such as rash, itching anus or vulva.

B. Musculoskeletal Reactions—headache, backache, cramps.

C. Respiratory Reactions—hyperventilation, asthma.

D. Cardiovascular Reactions—migraine, hypertension, chest pains.

E. Gastrointestinal Reactions—dyspepsia, ulcers, obesity, diarrhea.

F. Genito-urinary Reactions—menstrual dysfunctions, impotence, frigidity.

G. Endocrine Reactions—infertility.

H. Nervous System Reactions—chronic fatigue.

The Psychotic Reactions are as follows:

A. Schizophrenic Reactions—severe difficulty in interpersonal relations, withdrawal from reality, personality disorganization.

B. Affective Reactions—severe disturbance of affect with thought, behavior and mood changes, manic-depressive symptoms.

C. Involutional Reactions—depression with physical complaints, usually late in life.

D. Paranoid Reactions—ideas of persecution or grandiose delusions.

    1. Paranoid State—generalized oversuspiciousness.

    2. Paranoia—an encapsulated delusion with relatively normal functioning in other areas.

E. Organic Brain Disorders.

Levels of Dysorganization—The Downward Spiral

Some of the most common stresses which tend to precipitate emotional upset are marital conflicts, job problems, guilt feelings, and threats to the self-image.

Common early warning signs of emotional upset are:

1. Changes from usual behavior.

2. Anxiety and irritability.

3. Sleep disturbances.

4. Depression, withdrawal, comments about suicide.
5. Excessive drinking, not under the individual's control.
6. Sexual problems.
7. Excessive altercations.
8. Accident prone—physical or traffic accidents.
9. Argumentative—feeling persecuted.
10. Physical complaints of a chronic nature.
11. Excessive discussion of home problems.
12. Deterioration in work performance.
13. Loss of interest and self-confidence.

Menninger[13] has outlined the downward spiral to levels of dysorganization as one becomes emotionally upset.

1. First level—Slight impairment of control and some failure in coping, resulting in *nervousness*. Symptoms are a conscious effort at self-control. Inhibitions, exaggerated perception, tearfulness, over gaiety, restlessness, instability, worry, denial, minor somatic and sexual dysfunctions. This is a reversible or transitional state. Some cases recover, some get worse.

2. Second level—Development of neurotic level symptoms. There is subjective discomfort and anxiety—a sense of failure, uselessness, incompetence and of being a disappointment to oneself and others. Work becomes drudgery and friends seem perverse or provocative.

3. Third level—Outbursts of aggression and destructive impulses—assaults and social offenses. Indicates greater weakness than second level disturbances. This level is generally characterized by loss of control of aggressive impulses and lashing out, may be homicidal.

4. Fourth level—Abandonment of the will to live, psychological death, which may lead to successful suicide.

Skeletons From The Past

Missildine[15] describes the inner child of the past and how we are all influenced in varying degrees by our childhood experiences.

All too frequently unsatisfied childhood needs, frustrations and fixations remain active in us as adults and on an unconscious level tend to influence our behavior as if we are still living in the past. Many of these childhood needs are no longer appropriate. Environment has changed and our needs and capabilities as adults have changed as well.

In order to avoid the repetitive kinds of emotional conflicts that constitute the broken record syndrome, a person must come to terms with his old skeletons. This involves psychological separation from parents and the development of a self-image as equal and valuable adult to replace the old self-image of helpless, dependent, unequal child.

When this change is achieved, one should have the conviction of being on a par with any other adult regardless of the title or station in life. Equality is now measured in terms of human value rather than by status or material goods.

Another relic from the past which can cause serious difficulty is the internalized parent skeleton. This is the harsh, overly punitive conscience which is based on outmoded comparisons and values. This is the dinosaur skeleton that administers self-punishment and evokes depressive feelings, isolation and despair.

In order to open the closet and remove the skeleton, it is necessary to evaluate one's parents from the perspective of adult rather than from the vantage point of the child.

By seeing parents as fallible human beings who have weaknesses and faults, the old sense of awe and reverence can be replaced by a realistic acceptance of parents as people who are no better or no worse than most others. One can then reevaluate himself more realistically from the stance of equality toward other adults rather than from the position of inferiority.

Among men in police work, one of the common symptoms of the parent skeleton is the ambivalence felt toward people in authority. There is usually a mixture of reverence and awe toward high ranking officers along with underlying resentment and anger. This is reminiscent of the feeling that children have toward parents when they are vulnerable, helpless and resentful of their dependency.

BIBLIOGRAPHY

1. *Biological Rhythms in Psychiatry and Medicine.* National Institute of Mental Health, 1970.
2. Brodsky, Stanley: *Psychological Training Techniques in Law Enforcement and Corrections.* Center for Forensic Psychiatry, Ann Arbor, Michigan, 1970.
3. Cameron, Norman: *Personality Development and Psychopathology.* Boston, HM, 1963.
4. Cannon, Walter: *The Wisdom of the Body.* Norton, 1939.
5. *Emotions and Physical Health.* Metropolitan Life Insurance Company, 1959.
6. Fink, David: *For People Under Pressure.* New York, S & S, 1956.
7. Hilgard, Ernest R.: *Introduction to Psychology.* New York, Harcourt, Brace and World, 1962.
8. Hollander, E. P. and Hunt, Raymond: *Current Perspectives in Social Psychology.* Fair Lawn, Oxford U Pr, 1963.
9. Jersild, Arthur T.: *Child Psychology.* Englewood Cliffs, P-H, 1960.
10. Levi, Lennart: *Stress: Sources, Management and Prevention.* New York, Liveright, 1967.
11. Levinson, H.: *Emotional Health in the World of Work.* New York, Harp T., 1964.
12. Lewis, Howard R. and Martha E.: *Psychosomatics.* New York, The Viking Pr, 1972.
13. Menninger, Karl: *The Vital Balance.* New York, The Viking Pr, 1963.
14. *Mental Illness and Law Enforcement.* Law Enforcement Study Center, Washington University, 1970.
15. Missildine, W. Hugh: *Your Inner Child of the Past.* New York, S & S, 1963.
16. *Physical Fitness for Law Enforcement Officers.* Federal Bureau of Investigation, Washington, 1972.
17. *Recognizing and Supervising Troubled Employees.* U.S. Civil Service Commission, July, 1967.
18. Rodale, J. I. *Your Diet and Your Heart.* Emmaus, Rodale, 1969.
19. Selye, Hans: *The Stress of Life.* New York, McGraw, 1956.
20. Spitz, Rene: *The First Year of Life.* New York, Intl Univs Pr, 1965.
21. Storr, Anthony: *Human Aggression.* New York, Atheneum, 1968.
22. Watson, George: *Nutrition and Your Mind. The Psychochemical Response.* New York, Harp T, 1972.

CHAPTER FIVE

COUNSELING, THERAPY AND THE SUPERVISOR'S ROLE

MEN IN POLICE WORK commonly have a skeptical and suspicious attitude toward psychiatrists and psychologists. This feeling is frequently reciprocated by the mental health professional. Superficially it may appear as if these two professions have vastly different goals. However, on closer examination it becomes apparent that the goals are very similar in terms of helping people and improving society, but the techniques and means of achieving them may differ slightly.

The lack of factual information and unfamiliarity of one professional with the roles and functions of the other, increase suspicion and wariness. By working together on projects of mutual concern, by coordinating and sharing expertise, both professions can reduce apprehension and acquire a more realistic understanding and appreciation of each other.

THE MAGIC FORMULA

Belief in magic is normal in children, in dreams, and in psychotic states, but magical thinking also tends to persist in some adults. It is expressed in the desire for quick cures, for magical answers to complex problems, and for an omniscient prophet to lead us to the promised land. Much time and effort can be spent looking for the secret or the magic formula. However, in reality this kind of formula rarely exists.

The Shaman and The Shrink

In primitive societies many natural events are attributed to supernatural powers. Sacrifices are made to the powerful deities thought to control rain, crops, birth and death.

In pre-literate tribes the shaman is the witch doctor and holy man in charge of influencing these external events by using his magical powers. In acting as intermediary between the ordinary tribesman and a particular god, he may roll the bones, utter incantations, do a dance, make a sacrifice, or engage in other ritualistic activities which in his expertise, he determines to be relevant to the particular problem.

Because primitive peoples believe in the witch doctor and because belief systems are extremely important in influencing external as well as internal reality, the shaman is often successful in effecting a variety of cures. His rites and magical incantations are considered as up-to-date to the primitive person as the heart-lung machine is to a modern individual. So, both are believed in.

A *headshrinker* in our society occupies a position somewhat similar to the shaman. We impute to him magical powers, mind-reading ability and knowledge of the answers to all personal and interpersonal problems. Belief and trust are key factors in how successful treatment will be. Studies of therapists of various orientations have indicated that the particular school of thought is secondary to personal qualities, and background of experience in helping people.

If a psychologist from the United States were to visit a primitive tribe, his procedures would be seen as very strange, and it would likely result in his having very little effect on the problems of the primitive individual. Similarly, if the shaman tried to practice in our culture, his rolling of the bones and incantations would probably seem comical and ludicrous. Because of belief and trust, each seems to be more effective in his own society.[4]

Pills and Magic

Suggestion is a potent motivator and his significant influence on what we believe and how we react. This is exemplified in the millions of dollars spent on television commercials to influence people to buy tons of pills which are not really necessary and are frequently harmful. The effectiveness of suggestion can also be seen in the experiments using placebos, inert chemicals such as sugar pills which have *cured* people of specific maladies.

Whether in primitive or modern society, there is the tendency to invest with magical significance medicines and other things that we ingest orally. We hope for supernatural, magical answers to our problems and the charisma of the pill supplies that for us.

An increasing variety of pills appear on the market to take away ailments and to change our lives magically. Research is in process to discover pills to increase our intelligence, generate creativity, improve memory, and enhance learning.

Psychologically, magic derives from oral needs and the desire for soothing and satisfaction. As Roheim[9] points out, the almost universal cure-all of primitive medicine is sucking. Developmentally, this *mouth magic* gets transferred to the spoken word as the mother reacts to the child's uttered sounds and satisfies his desires.

Repeated reduction of tension reinforces the connection of getting gratified by the use of sounds—incantations or utterances. Love magic utilizes potions and bodily fluids which are believed to influence and to bring responsiveness from the loved one. One of the main functions of all magic is to counter feelings of helplessness and vulnerability by invoking omnipotent, supernatural mastery and control.

Insight and Flexibility

In counseling and therapy there is no magic. Rather there is an attempt to investigate the origins of certain conflicts and to look for ways of resolving them. With the assistance of the counselor, the person with a conflict develops awareness and insight into the origins of his anxieties, his confusion and his difficulty with coping.

As he gains more self-awareness, he can be less defensive since understanding leads to better control, less helplessness and isolation. With reduced defensiveness he can also be more flexible, and more open-minded since there is less perceived danger from the environment and from within. Greater flexibility lessens the likelihood of small amounts of stress or tension upsetting the established equilibrium.

COUNSELING AND THERAPY

The person in conflict is usually so immersed in and surrounded by emotions that he can's see the forest for the trees. This is reflected in the old maxim that the doctor who treats himself has a fool for a physician. The adult approach in dealing with severe emotional conflict situations is to consult a professional person who is uninvolved and more objective. To silently and stoically endure emotional pain is as silly as holding one's jaw and complaining about a toothache rather than picking up the phone and calling the dentist.

The Short and Long Of It

Counseling has been defined as assistance with personal types of problems not classified as illness. These include marital, job, social, or personality problems. Psychotherapy has been described as the treatment of personality disturbances, mental illnesses and the more serious psychological problems.

However, in practice, it is very difficult to distinguish between the two since there is considerable overlap. There are a variety of counseling and therapy approaches, some of which are short-term and others which take years to complete.

Counseling and psychotherapy both attempt to investigate and define the problems, to look for possible causes, and to work through the conflicts in order to modify the untenable situation.

In most cases, situational problems such as traumatic events or temporary stresses and pressures can be dealt with on a relatively short-term basis whereas established personality problems and chronic emotional upsets need more extensive work. In a brief crisis intervention approach, an attempt is made to rapidly resolve the precipitating conflict is one to six sessions.

In therapy where personality modification is one of the goals, a long-term psychoanalysis of three to five years, several times a week may be the treatment of choice. In counseling or in therapy the relationship between the client and counselor or therapist is very important. Much of the work that gets done is based on a cooperative therapeutic alliance. This puts a premium on personal compatability.

There is growing impatience today and a search for short-term, painless answers to personal problems. This has helped spawn a rash of fad-type therapies which promise titilation and instant happiness. Sadly, most of today's fads will be tomorrow's forgotten failures. It is hard to escape the reality that magical answers can't solve the complex problems of living.

How Change Occurs

Counseling and psychotherapy are essentially processes of relearning, which occur through the vehicle of the therapeutic relationship. By focusing on specific conflicts, fears and problems, the counselee can explore their origins, and connections can be made to significant events in one's life.

During the counseling process unconscious motives can be brought to awareness and dealt with more adequately. The therapist makes interpretations of events, statements and behavior of the client in order to link up diverse behaviors to make them more comprehensible. During counseling the client has the opportunity to unburden himself and re-experience intense emotional feelings which can afford him relief.

In the process of linking-up and bringing into awareness things that were outside of his conscious control, the client develops an insight into the roots of his conflict. However, in addition to insight a process of working-through is necessary. This involves facing the same conflicts repeatedly until he learns to confront them directly and to master them rather than employing ineffective defenses which inhibit and cripple.

Important areas commonly explored in the counseling process which affect optimal function are family, work, social life, self-concept, and handling of sexual and aggressive feelings.

One of the main reasons professional help is desirable for emotional problems is that many of the underlying factors are unconscious. In addition, defenses lead to self-deception which make it almost impossible to solve personal problems without objective help. Admission of one's problems and the desire to get help is a sign of emotional strength rather than weakness or inadequacy.

THE SUPERVISOR'S COUNSELING ROLE

It is now a well established fact that successful counseling is not primarily a function of advanced training in some technique, as has long been asserted, but that it is mainly a function of personality and basic character.[12]

The effective supervisor has a legitimate and necessary role in counseling. He is involved to some degree with the problems of his men whether he likes it or not because these problems exist. Denying them or turning away from them doesn't aid in handling the problems.

One of the difficulties the supervisor has as a counselor is his need to contain his own feelings, which can cause him tension and anxiety, and may make him feel that the counseling role is really not for him. On the other hand helping another adult person through adequate counseling can yield tremendous satisfaction.

Attitude—Help or Punish?

In our society the image of the real man is the strong, silent male, one who would rather cut off his right arm than cry. It also includes the notion that compassion and openness are sissy or soft. These attitudes exact a high price and are detrimental emotionally. The fact is that men are human with strong feelings and weaknesses as well as muscle strength. Admitting this doesn't make one less of a man.

The supervisor in a counseling role needs to develop a concept of psychological distance, of maintaining objectivity rather than reacting in a personal way. He knows the difference between empathy and sympathy.

Developing empathy is desirable in a counseling attitude because it allows you to briefly step into the other person's shoes and feel a little bit of what he is experiencing. This leads to a better understanding of his problem and improved communication. Sympathy, however, involves an attitude of superiority and looking down on an unfortunate inferior. This can set up a relationship based on helplessness versus strength which is inimical to the long-range goal of counseling: making the counselee stronger and more independent.

In avoiding overidentification with the person being counseled, the supervisor maintains his objectivity by being aware of *whose problem is it?* By reminding himself that it is not his problem being discussed, the supervisor can keep his own emotions and difficulties in the background and not confuse the counselee's.

The supervisor also needs to distinguish among his several

roles. He is aware that a policeman is a helper as well as an enforcer of laws and that a conflict may occur between these roles in certain situations. In this type of conflict, the use of discretion is legitimate and necessary in decision-making the professional policeman must engage in.

His own many roles include supervising, disciplining, counseling and that of fellow human being. The well-adjusted sergeant feels at ease in various roles and doesn't necessarily have to emphasize one to the exclusion of the others.

In counseling it is very helpful to have positive attitudes. This includes tolerance, understanding and responsiveness rather than a paternalistic or domineering approach.

The supervisor who has to remain in charge in the counseling role to show the client the error of his ways by acting like the stern parent is defeating himself in his counseling role. This attitude perpetuates the insecurity in the client by reinforcing his feeling that he isn't capable of making his own decisions and of behaving in a mature adult way.

The Interview Process

The physical setting for the personal interview in the counseling relationship is very important. Privacy is required rather than a coffee room setting where other people can overhear the conversation. The atmosphere should be informal and relaxed, preferably over a cup of coffee rather than the formal desk and chair arrangement.

The supervisor also avoids embarrassing anyone in public situations with comments about personal problems. When he encounters situations like this, he points out the inappropriateness of discussing personal matters publicly, or using a colleague for a scapegoat, or the butt of a joke.

In the interview he focuses on feelings and helps the person being counseled to express and release his feelings with as little difficulty as possible. By being at ease with emotional expression, he helps the individual to adopt a similar attitude toward his own feelings. He helps elicit the facts surrounding a particular problem situation which also aids the individual to ventilate and get things off his chest.

When the underlying factors are understood, he helps the counselee to look at possible alternatives or solutions to the problem. He is careful not to make decisions for the person. He clarifies, connects up and points out possibilities which the other person may not have been able to see because of his own emotional confusion.

Counseling Techniques

1. Directness and frankness is the best approach. Be yourself rather than trying to adopt an attitude of omnipotence or fatherly concern. The adequate supervisor does not beat around the bush but confronts difficulties when he becomes aware of them. His approach is not hostile or threatening, but a realistic encountering of the problem and the taking of appropriate steps to deal with it constructively.

2. Establish rapport by maintaining an attitude of equality rather than talking down or maintaining a superior position. This requires the ability to see the men as equal adults rather than as inferiors or subordinates.

3. Listen carefully. One of the hardest things for a counselor to do is to listen to what is being said with concentration and comprehension. The very act of listening does several things. It allows the person to ventilate or get some fresh air into his problem areas. It also provides him with ego support in that he now has an ally to share his burdens with, rather than going it alone. And third, by listening you are acting as a sounding board which the person can bounce his problems from permitting him to get some better understanding, insight, and increased control.

4. Reflect and clarify feelings. By rephrasing and restating important feelings, the counselor lets the client know that he is being listened to and understood. This also affords both the opportunity to clarify areas of confusion.

5. There is also a place for questioning. The supervisor, by carefully asking questions in a non-threatening way, can probe for underlying feelings that may not have come up spontaneously. The kinds of questions asked should be open-ended rather than ones that can be answered by a simple *yes* or *no,* which would

prevent feelings from being elicited. Questions should not be asked as in an interrogation, but with an attitude of interest and a desire to help. If done adequately, the client will not feel he is in the hot seat getting the third degree.

6. Reflective summary. After sufficient information has been assembled, feelings have been aired, and an understandable picture of the problem has been constructed, the counselor can summarize in simple terms his understanding of the situation based on what he has heard and interpreted. The person counseled can then add to, correct or modify any part of the summary in order to make it applicable and more acceptable to him.

Things to Avoid

1. Putting off confrontation—beating around the bush helps to build tension and magnify the importance of the conflict rather than reducing it.

2. Prejudging the person or situation. Avoid criticising or moralizing. The counselor's role is not to teach or lecture the individual, but to help him within his own frame of reference and capability.

3. Playing the mastermind. The counselor who has an attitude of omnipotence is going to reinforce the helpless feelings of his counselee. If he psychologizes, it is usually perceived as an intellectual put-down by the client who will react with underlying hostility and resentment.

4. Being too self-critical and fearful. The counselor should keep in mind that even professional mental health experts make mistakes. Therefore, he should not be too apprehensive about his own limitations in the counseling area. It is likely that the client will live in spite of minor errors or misinterpretations. If the relationship is a good one, mistakes can be overcome easily.

5. Transference problems. Because the counselor is in a helping role, he tends to symbolize to the client the magician who has all the answers, or the authority figure who may punish, forgive or criticize.

Invariably, the client unknowingly transfers onto the counselor some of his own feelings and conflicts from the past. For this reason, the counselor must be able to separate his professional role from his personal reactions. For example, if a client gets angry without real justification, the counselor should be aware that this can be a transference reaction not directed at him personally but at his symbolic authority. He can then feel comfortable in exploring this for his client's benefit.

Making a Referral

The counselor shouldn't try to be a junior psychiatrist. He needs to be aware of the limits of his expertise. He avoids getting into deep personality problems, and stays mainly with the reality difficulties related to job, family and social life. Ordinarily he limits his counseling help to a range of one to four sessions.

First, he needs to determine if there is an acute crisis, rather than a chronic situation of long standing which will require more professional help. He asks himself if brief counseling may help suffice in this situation, and then decides to counsel. However, he also needs to know when a referral is indicated.

Some immediate referral criteria:

1. Suicidal—Homicidal—Psychotic.
2. Inability to work and function routinely.
3. Specialized help needed—legal, financial, alcoholism, etc.
4. Evaluation of acting-out potential necessary.
5. Counseling time limits used.
6. Counselor has feeling that there is more than he can deal with.
7. In situations involving disability claims and workmen's compensation cases.

There are a few basic techniques in making a referral. The first is explaining the need and reasons for the referral. These should be realistic and should not reflect a desire to get rid of the client. The second is a *selling* of the referral. This helps reinforce the counselee's motivation to follow through.

The supervisor should be aware of the difference between a voluntary and a through-channels referral, including the understanding that a voluntary referral is confidential while a mandatory, through-channels type is not. After agreeing to the referral, the client should be assisted in getting connected. This can be done by making the initial phone call, setting up the appointment, and seeing that the referral gets implemented.

Finally, within the constraints of confidentiality, he should follow up the referral whenever possible to increase his own knowledge about the counseling problems and process and to indicate his interest in the counselee.

The supervisor should be familiar with counseling resources in the department and in the community. This includes fee scales, day and evening hours, health insurance coverage for inpatient and outpatient mental health problems, and types of treatment offered in the various clinics and private settings.

Knowledge of the procedures for making a referral, as well as such community resources as mental health clinics, hospitals, family service agencies, legal, child guidance clinics, welfare and recreational agencies, alcoholism councils, and financial assistance programs is useful. In many communities, a welfare information agency publishes a directory of the various services available which the counselor can use in referral situations.

In making an outside referral to a private practitioner, the counselor can use the referral service of the local psychiatric and psychological societies. Typically, the referral service gives the names of three qualified practitioners in the client's area.

In large police departments, the medical or personnel section usually maintains referral rosters of psychiatric and psychological consultants, as well as other specialists for referral in disability cases. If there is a specialized mental health or hospital detail, the assigned officers are usually familiar with community facilities and can facilitate hospitalization if this is necessary.

BIBLIOGRAPHY

1. Caplan, Gerald: *Principles of Preventive Psychiatry.* New York, Basic, 1964.
2. Erikson, Erik H.: *Identity and the Life Cycle.* Psychological Issues Monograph, 1959.
3. Hunt, Raymond: A concept of counseling for managers and work supervisors. *Professional Psychology,* pp. 236-242, Spring, 1970.

4. Malinowski, Bronislaw: *Magic, Science and Religion.* Garden City, Anch. Doubleday, 1955.
5. Menninger, William C. and Levinson, Harry: *Human Understanding in Industry—A Guide for Supervisors.* Science Research Associates, 1956.
6. Parad, Howard J. (ed.): *Crisis Intervention: Selected Readings.* Family Service Association of America, 1965.
7. Ramsey, Glenn: *Counseling Aids.* University of Texas, 1970.
8. Rogers, Carl R.: *Client-Centered Therapy.* Boston, HM, 1951.
9. Roheim, Geza: *Magic and Schizophrenia.* New York, Intl Univs Pr, 1955.
10. Sokol, Robert and Reiser, Martin: Training police sergeants in early warning signs of emotional upset. *Mental Hygiene,* pp. 303-307, July, 1971.
11. Tarachow, Sidney: *An Introduction to Psychotherapy.* New York, Intl Univs Pr, 1963.
12. Truax, C. B. and Carkhuff, R. R.: *Toward Effective Counseling and Psychotherapy: Training and Practice.* Aldine, 1967.

CHAPTER SIX

THE WORLD OF TEENAGERS

A MONG NON-LITERATE PEOPLES, the youth are ready to assume the status of adult at puberty or shortly thereafter.[18] In our culture the young adolescent is not considered adult. Marriage must be postponed and sexual experiences discouraged. Parents tend to maintain the adolescent state, providing little or no increase in responsibilities. These are a few of the factors causing increased conflict for the teenager, his parents and others.

WHO AM I?

An important problem facing the teenager is how to differentiate himself as a separate person and achieve adulthood in a system which prolongs dependency and withholds adult prerogatives. This creates and institutionalizes a developmental period during teenage which places the young person in an isolated category somewhere between child and adult.

Between Child and Adult

Childhood is a long period of dependency. The infant is relatively helpless and depends on parental care for its existence and satisfaction. Parents set careful limits to protect and nurture the small baby. As the child develops and becomes more capable, parents need to widen the limits accordingly so the child can test and experience his new found abilities and so continue to grow.

The child is also largely dependent on parents for his sense of self. In modeling himself after the adults in his environment, the

78

child internalizes some of their standards and behavioral traits. Over time these crystallize and become part of the child's self-image.

Puberty ushers in the stage of adolescence, with hormonal, physical, and psychological surges. The young adolescent still governed by childhood needs and habits, begins to feel a simultaneous desire to be grown up and to assume the prerogatives of adulthood. There is a tendency to vacillate between childlike behavior and adult sophistication.

Developmentally, this stage of life is turbulent, with strong feelings of confusion, inadequacy and self doubts. Underneath the turmoil is the central question, *Who am I?* In this regard, a major portion of adolescent conflict involves the problem of identity.

The Identity Crisis

Erikson[9] has attributed much of the identity crisis to role diffusion. In order for a person to develop an integrated personality as an adult, he must combine and synthesize the various separate, partial identifications which have been internalized. Much of the identity confusion in adolescence results from these diffuse roles not being integrated into a composite self-concept.

In order to develop an integrated personality, the adolescent has to unify his constitutional factors, basic needs, innate capacities, partial identifications, workable defenses and evolving roles. The internal process is also influenced by what other people think, depending on the composition and solidity of the self-image. The more that different environmental opinions influence the individual, the more his identity is buffeted by them.

The teenager's feelings of confusion, lack of direction and not knowing where he belongs, should get resolved by the end of teenage, with the development of a philosophy of life and a more comfortable sense-of-self. But during the working-through period, he is influenced from many directions to test out, to adopt trial identifications and to try on new roles to find out who he really is as a person. Whether these adventures are benign, harmful, or growth-inducing depends largely on earlier childhood experience and the resultant security system.

REBELLION AND DEPENDENCY

A teenager's main conflict centers around achieving independence and coming to terms with his long period of dependency as a child. Rebellion and negativism among teenagers are fairly typical defenses in our society.

Because parents represent the establishment and are connected with the dependency of childhood, they need to be pushed away from and gotten free of. This is a process of cutting the apron strings which allows the teenager to move from the child role to an adult role. The helpless dependency of childhood must be changed into the adult kind of mutuality wherein adults voluntarily give and take with each other as equals without playing parent and child.

Teenagers adopt fads in the rebellious push for independence. Group support is increased by the use of emblems which help identify the new unified subculture.

Fads—Dress, Hair and Objects

Teenage fads usually focus on clothing, hair styles, jewelry and language. Emblems, such as jackets, also provide status and in-group identification. Fads tend to have a periodic life cycle. Maintaining a fad or emblem too long tends to institutionalize it, which is what the teenager is fighting against.

The increased self-consciousness of the teenager is countered by a flaunting of the body, distinctive dress and the adopting of peer group values such as *let it all hang out.* Interestingly, the very sameness of the teenager's group conformity lends support to opposing the parents values which represent the establishment.

Group Pressure—The Gang

In cutting the apron strings within the family, the teenager makes a shift from home to outside environment. He rejects parental values and enlarges his social circle outside of the home. A high value is placed on peer group norms and expectations.

The group or gang becomes very important. His first loyalty is to the gang. In a choice between parents opinions and group values, the group usually wins out. Being an *in* member of the group is felt to be a matter of life and death to the teenager, because here he feels supported and recognized as a separate, independent person. At home, he is still the helpless, dependent child.

In addition to the satisfaction of belonging, the teenager gains group recognition and the opportunity to prove himself a real man. This involves various kinds of testing-out behavior, some innocuous and some illegal and harmful. Along with risk-taking and seeking danger is a shift from the use of thought to the use of muscles. The desire for body involvement and action increases the incidence of acting-out.

Acting-Out

The long period of childhood dependency leads to keeping feelings in, conforming to parents' desires and not being free to express aggressive feelings. With the movement away from home and parents during teenage, is also a tendency to express angry and violent feelings as well as sexual ones. This shift from a passive to an active mode changes the inner balance toward the environment.

The acting-out behavior of adolescence ranges from normal to symptomatic of emotional distress. The teenager who does not act-out at all may have as serious a problem as the teenager who acts-out his violent and sexual impulses.

The tendency to act-out is increased by the peer pressure and norms of the group. He feels support from the group and can minimize guilt feelings by sharing them among many members of the group. If everyone else is doing it, he doesn't have the major responsibility and so can go along as just one of the gang.

Idealism and Ideology

Teenagers are highly idealistic and prone to intellectualism. They want to know the reasons for things and frequently ask the question *Why?* In working through their identity confusion and trying to synthesize a viable self-concept, ideological issues are confronted. Typical of these are, *Is there a God?*, *Why am I here?*, *What is the meaning of the universe?*, and *What is my philosophy of life?* Finding acceptable answers to these questions is extremely important for the teenager if he is to successfully negotiate the rapids from child to adult.

TOWARD ADULTHOOD

If the teenager is to be successful in his development from the vacillations of adolescence to the maturity of adulthood, he must accomplish several crucial tasks.

Tasks To Be Achieved

The teenager has four main tasks to achieve in becoming an adult. The first is to move from dependency on parents and to establish himself as an independent individual. The second is to achieve a heterosexual adjustment. The third is to establish a vocational choice. Fourth is the achievement of emotional stability to face the problems of daily living, establishing of goals and a philosophy of life.

Emancipation from family and establishing independent functioning requires a positive self-image and an identity as an adequate adult person. This includes feelings of inner security, sexual adequacy, and equality with all other adults in the environment.

Heterosexual adjustment involves being attracted to and feeling comfortable with the opposite sex, and an absence of conflict and fear in heterosexual situations. The heterosexual relationship requires feelings of concern, tenderness and mutuality rather than a view of the partner as property or as an object for selfish satisfaction. An adult sexual relationship is based on equal give and take, mutual respect and value.

Developing a philosophy of life, establishing goals and directions is an outgrowth of one's sense-of-self. It includes insight into one's capabilities and shortcomings and putting them into some acceptable framework wherein needs can be satisfied and met. The vocational choice should capitalize on one's abilities and potentials. It should represent an interesting, challenging way of spending a large part of one's life.

Emotional stability involves coming to terms with oneself by resolution of the various conflicts that have been active during teenage, and answering the questions, *Who am I?*, *What am I worth?*, and *Where do I belong in this world?* All help to give a sense of security and stability.

Resolving the Conflicts

Many conflicts of teenage are part of the process and require time to be worked through. Testing-out, trying on new roles, chancing new situations, meeting new people, seeing oneself from different points of view, are all necessary maneuvers in achieving resolution.

Although some reduction of these conflicts is necessary in the course of becoming an adequate adult, complete and final answers aren't possible because self-questioning and growth continue throughout life. An adult is not a finished product, but a person in the state of becoming.

BIBLIOGRAPHY

1. Arnstein, Helene: *What to Tell Your Child.* New York, Bobbs, 1960.
2. Baruch, Dorothy: *New Ways in Discipline.* New York, McGraw, 1949.
3. Bettelheim, Bruno: *Love is Not Enough.* New York, Free Pr, 1955.
4. Blos, Peter: *On Adolescence.* New York, Free Pr, 1962.
5. Buxbaum, Edith: *Understanding Your Child.* New York, Grove, 1962.
6. *Campus Tensions: Analyses and Recommendations.* American Council on Education, 1971.
7. Lorand, Rhoda: *Love, Sex and the Teenager.* New York, Popular Lib, 1965.
8. De Ropp, Robert: *Drugs and the Mind.* New York, Grove, 1957.
9. Erikson, Erik: *Identity and the Life Cycle.* Psychological Issues, Monograph #1. New York, Intl Univs Pr, 1959.
10. Erikson, Erik (ed.): *The Challenge of Youth.* Garden City, Anch. Doubleday, 1963.
11. Feuer, L.: *The Conflict of Generations.* New York, Basic, 1968.
12. Fraiberg, Selma: *The Magic Years.* New York, Scribner, 1959.
13. Friedenberg, Edgar: *The Vanishing Adolescent.* New York, Dell, 1962.
14. Ginott, Haim: *Between Parent and Teenager.* New York, Avon, 1969.
15. Ginott, Haim: *Between Parent and Child.* New York, Macmillan, 1965.
16. Goodman, David: *A Parent's Guide to the Emotional Needs of Children.* New York, Pub by Hawthorn Arco, 1959.
17. Gordon, Thomas: *Parent Effectiveness Training.* New York, Wyden, 1970.
18. Mead, Margaret: *Culture and Commitment.* Garden City, Doubleday, 1970.
19. Piaget, Jean: *The Psychology of the Child.* New York, Basic, 1969.

20. Reiser, Martin and Kushner-Goodman, Sylvia: A drop-in group for teenagers in a poverty area, in *Adolescents Grow in Groups.* New York, Brunner-Mazel, 1972.
21. Reiser, Martin: A note on the analysis of the "Elvis Presley" phenomenon. *American Imago,* 1958, *15,* pp. 97-100.
22. *Shut it Down: A College in Crisis.* Staff Report, National Commission on the Causes and Prevention of Violence. U.S. Government Printing Office, June, 1969.
23. *The Adolescent in Your Family.* U.S. Department of Health, Education and Welfare, 1955.
24. Whitman, Howard: *Let's Tell the Truth About Sex.* New York, Monarch, 1963.
25. *Your Children and Their Gangs.* U.S. Department of Health, Education and Welfare, 1960.

CHAPTER SEVEN

DELINQUENCY AND THE CRIMINAL

WHAT IS CONSIDERED NORMAL or deviant behavior varies with different societies and subcultures. It also varies within the same individual depending on internal and situational stresses and social factors. Taking a towel or ash tray from a motel and distorting income tax returns are dishonest, but they are viewed as normal, acceptable behavior by many people in our society. Other examples of institutionalized deviant behavior include interesting gouging, deceptive business practices and fraudulent advertising.

WHAT IS DELINQUENCY?

Delinquency is a form of personal or social defense or adaptation which involves acting-out that is offensive or injurious to someone. It is sometimes difficult to distinguish delinquency from normal kinds of child and adolescent actions because behavior is on a continuum rather than simply right or wrong. While certain kinds of acting-out at Halloween may be considered normal, similar behavior at other times may be considered malicious mischief.

Types of Delinquency—Normal, Neurotic, Sociopathic

Although it isn't possible to categorize types of delinquency with accuracy and exclusivity, it is useful to view delinquency in a theoretical framework which can make it more understandable. There is considerable overlap among the various types of delinquency, but for purposes of discussion they can be classified into three kinds.

NORMAL—This delinquency involves the mischievous form of rebelling against authority and is usually recognized as fairly typical for the developmental level of those acting-out. The acts are usually petty offenses involving provocation, inconvenience or minor property damage rather than major injury. Characteristically, this type of delinquency does not involve a chronic behavior pattern.

NEUROTIC—This type of delinquency is a channel for discharging anxiety. The individual is able to function in life, but with considerable self-preoccupation and ego-constriction. He has guilt feelings over his misbehavior and is aware of the feelings and needs of other people, although his own needs come first. He has a faulty sexual identification which includes conflict with authority.

An extreme example of neurotic delinquency is the compulsive shoplifter who may have a pocketful of money but feels compelled to steal certain inexpensive items from a store because of his unconscious conflicts and needs. The items taken are symbolic of the affection and acceptance that were not given voluntarily by a significant person in the past. Because he is aware of reality and his guilt over misbehaving, the neurotic delinquent can be helped by a re-education process.

SOCIOPATHIC—This form of delinquency is associated with a character defect. A faulty conscience results in a lack of guilt feeling and poor social relationships with other people.

Typically, the sociopathic individual operates as a loner, independent of his environment and with little regard for the feelings and needs of other people. He has considerable underlying rage, resentment and anger against the world which severely cripples his ability to relate to others in a positive way.

The sociopathically motivated delinquent group is extremely difficult to work with. Because they view their behavior as acceptable, they have comprised the major failures in attempts at rehabilitation and correction. This recidivist group constitutes about 10 percent of the total number of people transiting the criminal justice system.

Because of the difficulty and lack of success with hardened sociopaths, psychiatrists, psychologists and other mental health professionals tend to shy away from involvement with this population. The rewards and working conditions have been minimal and the headaches great. This needs to be changed in future programming.

It is true that many people have a small amount of sociopathy and neuroticism and are able to function essentially within the normal range of behavior. The important question is how much of each component does a person have and what kind of balance exists in his personality which affects acting-out and offending others.

Some Characteristics of Delinquents

Chronic delinquents were very often severely deprived as children. Because of the trauma of brutal punishment, lack of affection and acceptance, the child develops defenses against possible hurt and influence by other people. The inner resentment and anger is then projected and generalized onto the whole world which is equated with the original source of deprivation. This results in a typical attitude of *The world owes me a living.*

The acts of delinquents often have a symbolic and magical quality about them as if the acting-out is a way of forcing the love and recognition they didn't receive when younger. The aggressive actions also provide feelings of omnipotence which eliminate the need for outside persons in order to achieve gratification.

A delinquent is able to master the trauma and satisfy his own needs in this magical way. At the same time, however, the underlying feelings of inadequacy and worthlessness persists, causing anxiety and insecurity. As a result, an overbalancing need to prove himself important emerges which involves serious risk-taking and life-threatening behavior. The need to prove his worth becomes a matter of life and death, and psychological survival. Thus the cycle of feeling inadequate and demonstrating manhood continues.

The chronic delinquent may behave in a coldly self-sufficient manner, seeming older than his years. He operates on the pleasure principle in needing immediate gratification of his desires rather than postponing and realistically working for longer range satisfaction. Therefore, if he wants something, he will take it.

Accompanying the feelings of inadequacy often is an unconscious need for punishment. He feels defective and responsible for his own lack of worth. The unconscious need for punishment may lead to repetitive, compulsive behavior in which the temporary pleasure in delinquent acting-out is followed by punishment or enhanced tension, which then increases the need for another act. In general, the chronic delinquent individual feels isolated and depersonalized to a large degree.

Interacting with the psychological factors involved in delinquent behavior, are social variables which are also important.

Normally, as a part of growing social development, group and gang behavior crystallize during the fifth or sixth grade. This ushers in a process of weaning from parental control and home environment by magnifying the importance of the peer group and conforming to in-group behavior. There appear to be some differences among socio-economic classes as to the degree of influence by peer groups, based on value systems and identification.

Lower class boys seem to have a greater need to demonstrate that they are not sissies in order to prove masculinity. Verbal challenges and confrontations are frequent as a way of testing-out of manliness and honor. In the value system of gangs, toughness, smartness, action and excitement have extremely high priority. There is a constant need to protect one's status in the gang, and this is done by asserting one's manhood.

Social delinquents frequently come from large families and also have siblings who are delinquent as well. It is not unusual for the parents of social delinquents to lack in setting a moral example or in using positive discipline techniques.

In large samples of children, good homes in bad environments can produce occasional nonserious delinquents who can be influenced to change rather easily. A poor home in a bad neighborhood environment is more likely to produce a socialized delinquent who rejects conventional standards in favor of the values of the subculture.

A more important factor seems to be the amount and kind of tension and conflict in a family situation. Conflict-laden homes in good or poor neighborhoods tend to produce serious misfits, particularly among only and oldest children, who seem to suffer most from parental disharmony.[41]

SOME CAUSES

There are numerous theories which attempt to account for delinquent behavior. A lively competition exists among social and behavioral scientists for the primacy of their views.

Genetic-Biological Theories

Research into the relationship between inherited traits and delinquent, criminal behavior has not yet proved any direct causal connections. Some of the early criminologists likened the primitive qualities of felons to apes and savages. Theories connecting physical defects, brain damage and body types, have been advanced over the years and the concept of the born criminal is still around today.

Recently there was considerable excitement over the XYY chromosome syndrome which supposedly was indicative of inherited criminal characteristics. However, subsequent research has largely discounted this theory.

The professional consensus today is that although genetic factors may well predispose an individual to certain behavioral patterns, environmental influences and early learning are deciding factors in the outcome.

Sociological Theories

Sociologists emphasize environmental factors in the causation of delinquency and minimize individual differences. Durkheim described *anomie* as a major factor. This is a state of frustration and depression resulting from social conditions which leads to loss of restraints and goals, and a feeling of being left out, of not belonging.

In the middle 1950's, Robert Merton's theory of deviance[31] led social scientists to strongly emphasize the importance of social variables. In the past ten years, delinquency prevention theory has stressed such social factors as housing, employment, social class and educational differences rather than individual pathology.

Subculture theory has been another popular sociological contribution.[49] This approach emphasizes the delinquent's identification with gangs and groups that differ from middle class standards. By being a part of a subculture, by rejecting middle class values with its morality and convention, the individual achieves status with his group. An important motive behind much delinquent behavior is the satisfaction in defying and upsetting representatives of authority, particularly the police.

Later sociological refinements of subculture theory explain gang behavior as a form of adaptation; a necessary kind of rebelliousness in circumstances where opportunities for *good* behavior are limited by society.[14]

In general, current sociological theories of delinquency tend to view criminal behavior as a natural, even constructive reaction to an adverse environment and social system.

Psychological Theories

The psychodynamic theories of delinquency emphasize the importance of emotional factors which affect early learning and personality development. Satisfaction of early basic emotional needs, including acceptance, recognition and affection lead to emotional security with minimal anxiety and a tendency toward honesty, warmth, and openness. Frustration of basic needs leads to varying degrees of insecurity, emotional coldness and character disturbances.

An important concept related to the development of insecurity and later delinquent behavior is deprivation. This involves either a lack or an excess of satisfaction of key needs. To feel secure, children need positive discipline and adequate setting of limits. As they develop, the limits need to be widened to allow for increased abilities and exercising of new skills.

Discipline that is largely punitive, lacking in warmth and consistency, can lead to defects in character. These defects are incorporated into the individual's personality as normal and acceptable. As a result, guilt isn't experienced when acting-out is based on these values.

The individual who is emotionally mature is able to empathize, give affection, and remain tolerant, cooperative and idealistic. These qualities are noticeably lacking in strongly sociopathic individuals.

An Overview

Obviously, a person is a composite of all the factors discussed, genetic, biological, sociological and psychological. To emphasize any one of these parameters to the exclusion of the others is unrealistic. A human being is the sum total of all of these variables in the particular combinations, amounts and interactions at any point in time. To be comprehensive, explanations of delinquent or criminal behavior must take all of these dimensions into account.

PREDICTING DELINQUENCY

There have been numerous attempts to find early predictors of delinquency so that high risk individuals might be identified. However, most of these studies have raised more questions than they have answered.

The Harvard Studies

Sheldon and Eleanor Glueck of Harvard are perhaps the most well-known researchers in the prediction of delinquency. In their twenty-year study on one thousand delinquents, they found that 78 percent of men released from better reformatories continued criminal activity, that 88 percent of delinquents continued their delinquent behavior and that delinquency rates drop for people in their late twenties. This suggests that maturation may accomplish what social institutions find difficult to do for a large number of individuals.[18]

The Gluecks developed a five-point social development table which they say can significantly discriminate potential delinquents as early as age six or seven. The five predictors of delinquency are: (a) discipline of the boy by the father (with overstrictness having negative affects), (b) supervision of the boy by the mother (with under-supervision having negative effects), (c) affection from the father, (d) affection from the mother, (e) cohesiveness of the family.

There is considerable controversy over the correctness of these findings, and numerous research studies are underway attempting to discover what the predictive validity is. If it should prove useful, it could open the door to a whole range of preventive strategies in minimizing delinquent behavior. These approaches would have to be scrupulous in not contravening constitutional rights of families and individuals.

THE CONTINUUM OF CRIMINAL BEHAVIOR

Most people have some potential for criminal acting-out behavior. In ordinary circumstances this tendency is controlled or expressed in socially acceptable ways. It is important to recognize criminal behavior not as an either/or situation, but as a range of possibilities from mild deviance to violent destructive behavior against people and property.

Aggression appears to be innate in humans as well as in lower animals. Active and aggressive moves are necessary for survival in confronting the environment. But the expression of anger, resentment and hostility is a function of personality development, learning and social controls in particular life situations.

The usually cool, calm police officer may be moved to lose control and act-out violently if he finds his wife in bed with another man. Almost instantaneously, his status can change from upholder of the law to criminal because of the triggering effect of emotion on aggressive drives. In evaluating criminal behavior, it is important to look beyond surface behavior to unconscious motives as well.

The Professional

Professional criminals constitute a relatively small proportion of all people who commit crimes. Professional criminals are out to make money and have chosen crime as the occupation best suited to their needs and talents. An illegal occupation is chosen over a legitimate one because it does not require competition or the postponement of gratifications. It also gives the feeling of being powerful and in control of the environment rather than being controlled by employers and others.

The professional criminal may see himself as a businessman, who tries to calculate the odds and is willing to take chances as long as he feels his chances are favorable. He gets a tremendous amount of satisfaction getting away with something, in upsetting the establishment, particularly the police. Frequently, he will see his way of life as a game in which he tries to outwit those in law enforcement who are opposed to him. When he loses, he is often philosophical about it rather than attempting a showdown.

Unconsciously the police represent parent figures while the criminal is a rebellious child who is out to thwart the parents and have his own way. The criminal prides himself on being cool, unemotional and proficient. He may spend a long time planning a particular crime and may show considerable ingenuity and even brilliance in his operation. Today many of the professional criminals are part of an organization in which a code of conduct has been institutionalized much in the same way that delinquent gang behavior is.

Many of the so-called professionals who hire themselves out to murder on contract are extremely disturbed individuals who may be latently psychotic as well as sociopathic in personality.

Another category of the professional criminal is the con-man who develops elaborate schemes for fooling people, besting the establishment, and making money for himself. This can range from a *pigeon-drop*, to floating bogus stocks for a nonexistent goldmine. Through the years there have been reports of schools operating to train people in shoplifting, pickpocketing and in various con games. Other *professionals* operate in the areas of smuggling, gambling, prostitution, narcotics, counterfeiting, forgery and bunco.

White Collar Criminals

White collar crime has been defined as a violation of the criminal law by a person of the upper socioeconomic class in the course of his occupational pursuits. These crimes are engaged in primarily by business and professional men. Frequently, if a statute is not actually violated, there are questions of ethics and morals that border on illegality. White collar crime can involve an individual or a corporation such as in medical quackery or price fixing.

It is estimated that medical quackery brings in a billion dollars a year for cancer cures, miracle machines and gadgets. An investigator for the American Medical Association proposes six rules for spotting the quack.[17]

    A. If he uses a special machine or formula and claims to cure diseases.

    B. If he guarantees a quick cure.

    C. If he advertises or uses case histories or testimonials to sell his cure.

    D. If he proclaims loudly for medical investigation and recognition.

    E. If he asserts that medical men are persecuting him or are afraid of his competition.

    F. If he says that surgery, or X-rays or drugs cause more harm than good.

Some of the types of white collar crimes engaged in by individuals and corporations include fraudulent conversion, conspiracy to defraud, falsification of accounts, forgery, embezzlement, tax evasion, infringement of patents, and violation of anti-trust laws. In the medical area some common offenses are fee splitting, unnecessary operations, and selling narcotics.

The white collar crime areas which have gotten the most attention recently are concerned with consumer affairs and consumer protection. Federal, state and local governments have set up consumer protection bureaus where citizens can report incidents of being cheated or being taken advantage of.

Questionable practices and crimes in consumer areas have included shoddy home improvement work, actual fraud or misrepresentation in repair of television, automobile and appliances, misrepresentation of investments, including land, stock and business franchise swindles. Excess interest charges, deception in written contracts and warranties, bargain sales of inferior merchandise, misrepresentation in advertising, sale of dangerous food, short weights, or untested drugs such as Thalidomide are all common practices falling into the area of white collar crime.

Although the police officer has traditionally seen himself catching criminals such as the robber, rapist, burglar and child molester, he has not identified himself too closely with the whole area of consumer frauds. This will likely become necessary as the definitions of crime are modified to include broader protections for the average citizen.

Crimes Against Persons and Properties

The FBI has reported that on the average of nine times a day during 1971, banks were robbed. The 3,285 assaults made during robberies, burglaries and larcenies represented an 8.5 percent increase over 1970. The 2,586 bank robberies in 1971 represented a 10.9 percent increase over the previous year.

The incidence of juvenile delinquency has shown a dramatic increase over the years with the highest rise in the cities followed by the suburban and rural areas. During a recent eight-year period, the incidence of increase in arrest of youngsters under eighteen was double the increase in adult arrests. It is predicted that this growing rate of crime will continue, with one out of every six boys ending up in court on other than a traffic offense sometime before his eighteenth birthday.

Boys are most often sent to juvenile court for committing larceny, burglary, motor vehicle theft, truancy and ungovernable behavior. Girls are most often sent to court for running away, larceny, sex offenses and incorrigibility. Apart from the harm to victims of delinquent acts against person or property, juvenile crime costs the nation an estimated four billion dollars annually.[24]

Because we value human life and dignity over property in our society, crimes against persons are considered more serious. The ability to identify with others, to experience feelings and concern about living things is a mark of higher level development. Those individuals who have either not developed or who have suppressed their feelings toward people, tend to emphasize the importance of material objects.

The patterns of criminal behavior frequently appear at a very early age. In youngsters who begin a style of acting-out that involves injuring animals, progressing to injuring peers, and setting fires, the likelihood is great that later they will commit bizarre, or extremely serious crimes against persons. Although property represents people symbolically, it is more easily repaired or replaced.

Many of those who commit the most violent offenses are chronic offenders. There is also a relationship between socioeconomic level, seriousness and chronicity of offense. Non-whites have higher rates than whites for assaults, property offenses and robbery. The one-time criminal is involved in fewer index offenses compared to the repeater.[7]

Sex Offenders

In trying to understand sex offenders and what makes them tick, it is useful to review the process of normal sexual development. Humans go through a series of growth stages which include two important developmental parallels, sex drive and object relations.

In the beginning, sexual impulses are autoerotic and object relations are narcissistic. Generalized body stimulation and a polymorphous perverse orientation is the underpinning, with succeeding emphases on oral, anal, phallic and genital satisfaction. Each stage overlaps the next as the individual develops.

If he reaches sexual maturity, the individual has advanced from a narcissistic preoccupation to a desire to relate to other people, to feel tenderness, concern, consideration and love toward his sexual partner. His sexual orientation is heterosexual, involving genital intercourse. He is willing to postpone his own needs if necessary in order to please his loved one. This is in contrast to the immature individual who remains fixated at an earlier developmental level with a primary concern of self-satisfaction, and an inability to relate significantly to someone outside himself.

The individual who progresses successfully through the various stages of sexual development, identifies strongly with his own sex resulting in a feeling of inner security and self-confidence. He has achieved a positive self-image.

The concepts of fixation and regression are important in comprehending sex offenders. Fixation involves getting stuck at an early level of development which results in an intensification of that stage. Traumatic events usually lead to fixation. An example would be early oral deprivation resulting in fixation where the individual can relate sexually only by using the mouth. This is opposed to the normal individual who also gets oral satisfaction in eating and drinking but doesn't use the mouth exclusively in an exaggerated way.

The more fixations an individual has the more likely he is to experience difficulty under stress and regress back to these early fixation periods. Regression is a retreat to these early points in sexual development because of tension or stress. This process includes a tendency to fantasize or act-out in the mode appropriate to the earlier sexual level.

Sex offenders include young, old, wealthy and poor. Situational factors also play a role. The difference between a charge of statutory rape and another decision can hinge on the time a girl's parents get home unexpectedly. Deviant sex offenders generally have underlying emotional conflicts and poor self-control. The behavior may involve brain damage, retardation or senility as a motivating factor.

Sexual perversions are acts which may be considered normal when part of the foreplay during sexual intercourse, but when used as a basis for exclusive satisfaction, particularly in public, are offensive to society. Some of these acts may include violent hurtful behavior either physically or psychologically.

There are several groups of sex offenders ranging from those who act-out in a mild non-threatening way to those who are highly dangerous to others. Usually considered more of a nuisance than a danger are those who exhibit themselves, the voyeur or peeping tom, the transvestite or *drag queen,* or the consenting homosexual adult in a private setting.

Another group of sex offenders are those who act-out under a variety of stresses which may include personal stress, influence of drugs or alcohol, or isolation which precludes normal sexual outlet.

A different group are those whose acting-out is anti-social and related to criminal behavior. This might include gang rape, rape during a robbery, or sexually perverse activities incident to a crime.

A different category of offenders are those whose behavior is chronic and compulsive, which may involve violent or aggressive acts. These acts can include sex murder, sadistic mutilations or practices, violent activity involving children, and repeated rapes.

The majority of sex offenders have some previous record for a sex offense. In most instances the sexual offense is with someone known to the offender rather than a complete stranger. Many of the difficult-to-help sex offenders are not particularly dangerous to other people. The exhibitionist, the peeping tom, the transvestite are usually basically inhibited individuals who are afraid of adult relations with the opposite sex. They are sexually immature people who have fixations at early developmental points.

Policemen spend time and manpower policing public homosexual activity. With the emphasis on civil rights and the advent of numerous militant *gay* groups, homosexual behavior has become more acceptable when it is in private between consenting adults. However, the compulsive public homosexual engaging in aggressive or seductive behavior with young people remains a law enforcement problem.

Drug Offenders

We are a drug-oriented society, with large segments of our population using drugs in an attempt to cope with all kinds of physical, psychological and sociological discomfort. We are bombarded daily by television, newspaper and magazine advertisements which convince and condition us to desire a tension-less, stress-free existence. However, the business of living and interacting involves an inherent amount of stress and tension.

Drugs by themselves are not the culprit, people needing to abuse them are. Any single drug is potentially dangerous for some people, at a particular dosage, under certain circumstances. There is also a significant difference between the casual experimenter and the habitual abuser.

A few of the many reasons students are motivated to take drugs include curiosity, rebelliousness, to be more sociable, to find meaning in life, to have an exhilarating experience, or to reduce anxiety. Smoking cigarettes, drinking alcohol, using LSD or marijuana have become symbols of flouting authority and the establishment.

Only presenting the facts about drugs will not necessarily change behavior or attitudes. It depends on the context and how the facts are presented. Direct attacks on attitudes or behavior may serve to arouse further resistance and defensiveness. Attitude change usually involves personal experience and emotional involvement.[35]

A term often used in connection with drug use is habituation. The mild drugs that most people have had some experience with are contained in tobacco, tea, coffee and candy. Developing a habit is mainly the result of a psychological need. Addiction involves psychological dependence, but there is a physical need for the drug in addition. Other factors which influence drug taking are, what the person expects the drugs to do for him, and who is involved in sharing, giving, or administering the drug.

Drug abuse can be divided into three areas: legal, medical, and social. Legal abuse is defined in statutes. Medical abuse involves misuse of drugs in a clinical situation. Social abuse involves psychological factors. There are socio-psychological variables which may predispose some persons to become dependent on drugs. The exact category of drugs used may be incidental.

The most abused drug in our society today is alcohol. It ranks number three among national health problems with an estimated 4½ percent to 5 percent of all adult citizens in society classified as alcoholics. Approximately 75 percent of the population use alcoholic beverages and alcoholism also affects more than 700,000 women. The cost to industry of alcoholism is over four billion dollars annually.

Although there are theories about the causes of alcoholism, from organic disease to a lack of will power, the majority of people questioned by public opinion polls consider alcoholism a result of psychological problems. There is much ambivalence about alcoholism. Physicians publicly state that alcoholism is a medical disease, yet in their private practice frequently treat it as a character weakness. This gets communicated by negative feelings toward the alcoholic, usually including rejection.

Marijuana (cannabis) is still under scientific investigation to determine what the short and long range effects are on users. Although some present evidence suggests that cannabis does not produce short range harm to the individual's physical or mental well-being,[11] other studies are less benign. Obviously, further long-range research is necessary.

Other common classes of drugs in use by abusers are heroin,

cocaine, hashish, barbiturates, the amphetamines, hallucinogens, and inhalants. Although addiction itself is not a crime, drug abusers are crime-prone people.[43]

Some of the risks in drug abuse include psychosis, suicide, undesirable personality changes, release of sexual and aggressive impulses which may lead to murder, rape, homosexual episodes, habituation, hallucinatory experiences after drug taking has ceased, development of interest in other illicit drugs, developing of cult interest, warping of ordinary social outlooks, reduced work and social effectiveness, divorce and increased accident risk.

Medical personnel are especially prone to addiction and have a rate thirty times higher than that of the normal population. Demerol is said to be the primary drug abused. The choice of drug varies by class and subculture with heroin being the drug choice of lower classes whereas morphine and similar drugs are used by higher status people.

Those who become addicted to drugs usually have a predisposition based on abnormal dependency needs. Some of the dependency problems are reflected in personality in traits which include a lack of initiative and self-reliance, passivity, inadequacy and immaturity.

Conflicts specific to the adolescent addict in deprived urban areas are expressed in symptoms of limited emotional responsiveness, withdrawal under stress, lack of close relationships with others, oversensitivity to rejection, general unhappiness, difficulty in sexual identification and poor interpersonal abilities. In general, addicts have the same intelligence level as others but are operating at a reduced level of efficiency.

The President's Commission Report of 1967 concluded that the bulk of addicts were from deprived social groups and suffering from personality maladjustments. It found that individual motives and circumstances differed, but that most of the addicts lacked vocational skills, economic opportunities and personality strengths. They were oriented toward short range gratification from drugs rather than long term life goals.[43] It has been suggested that drug addiction is a long-term destructive, suicidal behavior.

Violent crimes attributed to users of cocaine probably involved loss of judgment and heightened aggression which, when combined with paranoid ideation, resulted in acting-out behavior against people.

The Task Force report on drugs found that ingestion of any mind altering substance by people with inadequate personalities from substandard social environments will increase the likelihood of deviant and criminal behavior. The causes of this behavior are to be found in the person and his environment rather than in the drugs themselves.

Most of the drug-related criminal behavior occurs among persons in large urban areas from lower class backgrounds, who are mostly heroin and alcohol abusers. Those addicts who do not come from large city slums or unintegrated groups usually have severe psychological disturbances reflecting early family disruption. The link between social and psychological disorders, drug abuse and subsequent dangerous behavior under drugs is very strong.

The latest estimate of the number of heroin addicts in the United States is five hundred to six hundred thousand. With all of the treatment programs, currently, less than 5 percent of drug addicts are successfully rehabilitated.

In 1971 an estimated three hundred million dollars in illegal narcotics was used in Los Angeles of which the police picked up only 20 percent. Street heroin is only approximately 3 percent pure as opposed to the 90 to 95 percent pure heroin available in Viet Nam.

Recently, it has been recognized that barbiturates constitute an even greater hazard than hard narcotics such as heroin. Addiction to barbiturates is harder to overcome, with withdrawal symptoms being more severe and even deadly. There are numerous incidents of *accidental* suicides where people on barbiturates also take alcohol, which potentiates the effect of the barbiturates resulting in a toxic overdose reaction.

Because of the difficulty in eliminating drugs from the market, the prevention approach has to be made effective. The threat of punishment alone is inadequate when people need help in developing alternative ways to cope with their problems. One effective approach is the educational where factual material is disseminated by a knowledgeable person of authority. He must know the drug scene, not be dogmatic or moralistic and present the information with the attitude that the individual must decide for himself whether or not to use drugs.

Although the success rate for treating heroin addicts has not been very great, addiction can be cured in some cases. In emergency situations when policemen are confronted by drug abusers or drug reactions, the first consideration should be getting qualified medical help. There are two broad categories of drug reactions, those directly from the drug, and extra-drug reactions.

In the first case the reaction is due to the specific drug, such as an overdose resulting in a comatose state. In extra-drug reactions the person's response is influenced by variables other than the drugs. These include the person's mental and physical state, the setting in which the drug was taken and the individual's expectations about the drug. Bizarre behavior, dangerous acting-out or panic reactions can result from any of the drugs depending on expectations as well as on the chemical effect of the drug itself.

Some of the current treatments available for drug abuse include long-term psychotherapy in individual or group settings, traditional treatment under confinement with an occupational and counseling approach, chemotherapy involving substitute drugs such as methadone, and self-help programs such as Synanon. All may be of use in a particular situation.

Although the police officer does not directly get involved in the treatment of drug abusers, his knowledge of the various treatment programs in the community will enable him to be more effective in making referrals and in discussing factually and knowledgeably the current state of affairs with drug use and abuse.

CORRECTIONS

Nationwide, our past attempts at rehabilitating or altering criminal behavior with traditional means of institutionalization have failed. There is currently renwed interest in examining the reasons for the failure and in reshaping the approaches and techniques used.

In modifying the process, it is important to consider the total criminal justice system, law enforcement, courts, probation, and prisons. All have impact on the success or failure of the rehabilitation concept.

The police very often feel frustrated when they see the courts releasing felony suspects and identified criminals who have an established pattern of destructive behavior. They also see hardened criminals being paroled and put back on the streets without adequate supervision and without having basically changed their value systems or tendencies toward criminal acting-out. While the public seems to agree that the corrections system is presently inadequate, there is a persistent lack of unity, enthusiasm, direction and eagerness to bring about positive changes.

The Prison Dilemma

There is almost unanimous agreement that our prison system is hopelessly inadequate and outmoded. Theoretically, individuals are sent to prison to teach them a lesson, to have them become re-educated in attitudes and value systems so that when they emerge they will be able to start over and be reintegrated into society as *normal* citizens.

To accomplish this the prison concept removes the individual from his community, takes away his personal identity and legal privileges, and has him *do time* as a way of paying for his transgressions. The outcome is supposed to have the individual recognize the error of his ways and change in a more positive direction. However, the data seems to suggest that this theory does not in fact work. There is a 65 to 80 percent recidivism rate among those who are sent to prison. Apparently the lesson is not learned, re-education does not occur, and the individual's value system is not changed in a more positive direction.

With the present focus on the failure of the penal system and a recognition of the need for more constructive approaches, many of the basic assumptions and theories of penology are being re-examined. Can criminals be rehabilitated? If so, what techniques can be used to accomplish this? How long will it take? What kind of personnel are required? What are the measures of success?

The basic function of a prison is to accomplish three things. First, to remove the individual from society so that he can no longer harm himself or anyone. Secondly, to impose external controls or constraints on him since he has shown his inability to use self-control. These two functions remain. The third facet of the prison experience, that of rehabilitation, or correction, is where the failure has been.

For most individuals in prisons, rehabilitation requires re-education or relearning at various experiential levels. This may range from the need for deep personality change in those individuals who have severe character disturbances or personality problems to more social forms of learning including the vocational, interpersonal and attitudinal.

At the present time there is a core of about 10 to 15 percent of sociopathic criminal types who are not being reached by current medical, psychological or educational techniques. To release these individuals into the community without alteration is to sacrifice the rights and needs of the community to those of one individual. In order to protect society against this relatively small group of deviant individuals, long-term institutional control should be required until more effective change processes can be developed.

For the rest of the population who are involved in the criminal justice system as offenders, there are currently available sufficient programs, techniques, and methods for helping them become reintegrated into society. However, what is urgently required is an effective assessment technique to sort out those who are accessible to assistance and those who are not. This would include a massive research program on a nationwide basis to test out and comparatively validate a wide variety of diagnostic and treatment programs.

Although prisons will likely continue to be necessary in the future, the character of the prison will have to change considerably. Those in control of the institutions will need to develop positive attitudes and expectations toward those who are incarcerated. Opportunities for self and formal education will have to be increased.

In order to reduce the reinforcement of homosexual behavior which is fostered by the closed setting in prisons, there should be an emphasis on family life education, family visits, conjugal weekends and on the positive potentials of the individual.

Problems in Parole

Parole and probation are useful concepts when not misused or abused. There are a number of offenders who are not particularly dangerous or fixed in their behavior who may be guided and supervised into more respectable channels and pursuits. However, this requires adequate manpower for supervision, for referral and for providing models to identify with.

A large percentage of the people who come in conflict with the law are alienated, have difficulty in socialization, are insecure, overdependent and have a poor image of themselves. One of the ways that values can be modified is by having an idealized role model in close contact with the individual who he can pattern himself after and emulate. This requires high calibre well-compensated professionals working in the area of parole.

These offenders who have committed serious crimes against persons such as rapes, homicides, and aggravated assault, should be paroled only under the closest supervision and after the most stringent psychological assessment. In borderline cases, the rights of society should have precedence over the possible loss of the individual's rights in a particular case. This is the hard value judgment that has permitted people to live together in social groups over the ages.

PREVENTION AND TREATMENT

The traditional role of the police officer is to catch the bad guy and put him out of circulation. However, because much of the crime problem is a result of social ills which have been increasing at a geometric rate, the policeman is playing a losing game. Prison becomes a revolving door, and combined with unrealistic probation practices, the officer finds himself catching the same person over and over. It is pretty much agreed by law enforcement administrators and by behavioral scientists that early prevention is necessary if crime is to be reduced and if policemen are to become more effective in their role in the community.

Early Prevention

Early prevention involves impacting those variables which ultimately result in the development of deviant or criminal behavior.

These factors include poor environmental conditions and difficulties in early family life which have later implications for emotional disturbance and disrupted social relationships. Improving housing, income, employment, educational opportunities and social status are all areas needing thoughtful consideration in attempts at early prevention.

Another of the important needs in prevention is an educational program to teach people how to be effective parents and how to deal with the needs of children which significantly effect later social-psychological development. Some of the child advocacy programs tentatively proposed may be a start in this direction.

Later Prevention

Ideally, early intervention is most desirable. However, this is not always possible in real life. There will always be individuals who will develop deviant or criminal behavior resulting in contact with the criminal justice system. In these instances, intervention is desirable at the earliest point possible in order to prevent a fixed pattern which may be impossible to reverse. These interventions can be arranged very early in childhood through school or health personnel, family members, or community caretakers who become aware of particular problems that have dire implications for the individual's future.

The later interventions usually require some form of treatment. Family counseling, individual therapy, group counseling, behavior modification, hypnotherapy, and recreational therapy are all possibilities for assisting individuals in altering behavior when symptoms of deviance have already appeared. Comprehensive research is necessary to compare and contrast various treatment methods to maximize assessment and referral outcomes.

BIBLIOGRAPHY

1. Becker, H.: *Outsiders: Studies in the Sociology of Deviance.* New York, Free Pr, 1963.
2. Brodsky, Stanley: *Psychologists in the Criminal Justice System.* American Association of Correctional Psychologists, 1972.
3. Caplan, Gerald: *An Approach to Community Mental Health.* New York, Grune, 1961.

4. Clor, Harry: *Obscenity and Public Morality.* Chicago, U of Chicago Pr, 1969.
5. Conrad, John: *Crime and its Correction.* Berkeley, U of Cal Pr, 1967.
6. *Corrections, 1968, a Climate for Change.* Joint Commission on Correctional Manpower and Training, August, 1968.
7. Cressey, Donald and Ward, David: *Delinquency, Crime and Social Process.* New York, Harp T., 1969.
8. *Crime and Delinquency Research in Selected European Countries.* National Institute of Mental Health, 1971.
9. Dieckmann, Edward and Mahendy, William: *Practical Homicide Investigation.* Springfield, Thomas, 1961.
10. Dressler, D.: *The Practice and Theory of Probation and Parole.* New York, Columbia U Pr, 1959.
11. *Drug Abuse and Law Enforcement.* Washington University, St. Louis, 1970.
12. *Drug Dependence.* National Institute of Mental Health, June, 1970.
13. Eissler, Kurt: *Searchlights on Delinquency.* New York, Intl Univs Pr, 1949.
14. Empey, LaMar and Lubeck, Steven: *Delinquency Prevention Strategies.* U.S. Department of Health, Education and Welfare, 1970.
15. Garabedian, Peter and Gibbons, Don (eds.): *Becoming Delinquent.* Chicago, Aldine, 1970.
16. Gebhard, Paul, et al: *Sex Offenders. An Analysis of Types.* New York, Harp T., 1965.
17. Geis, Gilbert (ed.): *White Collar Criminal.* New York, Atherton, 1968.
18. Glueck, Sheldon and Glueck, E. T.: *Ventures in Criminology.* New York, Pub. by Tavistock B & N, 1964.
19. Greenberg, Henry and Winters, Wallace: *About Mind-Altering Drugs and the Brain.* The Rotary Club of Pacific Palisades, California, 1971.
20. Halleck, Seymour: *Psychiatry and the Dilemmas of Crime.* New York, Harp T., 1967.
21. Hoffer, A. and Osmond, H.: *The Hallucinogens.* New York, Acad Pr, 1967.
22. Hollister, Leo: *Chemical Psychoses.* Springfield, Thomas, 1968.
23. *Juvenile Delinquency and Youth Crime: Task Force Report.* U.S. Government Printing Office, 1967.
24. *Juvenile Delinquency and Planning.* U.S. Department of Health, Education and Welfare, and Justice Department, Government Printing Office, 1971.
25. Karpman, Benjamin: *The Sexual Offender and His Offenses.* New York, Julian, 1954.
26. Kling, S.: *Sexual Behavior and the Law.* New York, Geis, 1965.
27. Kobetz, Richard W.: *The Police Role and Juvenile Delinquency.* International Association of Chiefs of Police, 1971.

28. Lerman, Paul (ed.): *Delinquency and Social Policy.* New York, Praeger, 1970.
29. Lindesmith, A. R.: *The Addict and the Law.* Bloomington, Ind U Pr, 1965.
30. Menninger, Karl: *The Crime of Punishment.* New York, Viking Pr, 1968.
31. Merton, Robert K.: *Social Theory and Social Structure.* New York, Free Pr, 1957.
32. Pooley, R. C., et al: *A Manual for Delinquency Intervention Counselors.* Center for the Study of Crime, Delinquency and Corrections. So. Illinois University, September, 1970.
33. Pursuit, Dan, et al: *Police Programs for Preventing Crime and Delinquency.* Springfield, Thomas, 1972.
34. Rapaport, A. and Chemmak, A.: *Prisoner's Dilemmas: A Study in Conflict and Cooperation.* Ann Arbor, U of Mich Pr, 1965.
35. *Resources Book for Drug Abuse Education.* U.S. Department of Health, Education and Welfare, October, 1969.
36. Roche, Philip: *The Criminal Mind.* New York, F S & G, 1969.
37. Rubin, Ted: *Law as an Agent of Delinquency Prevention.* U.S. Department of Health, Education and Welfare, 1971.
38. Schur, Edwin: *Our Criminal Society.* Prentice-Hall, 1969.
39. *Sexual Deviancy and Law Enforcement.* Law Enforcement Study Center. Washington University, 1970.
40. Springer, John: *Consumer Swindlers . . . and How to Avoid Them.* Chicago, Regnery, 1970.
41. Steel, Ronald (ed.): *New Light on Juvenile Delinquency.* Bronx, Wilson, 1967.
42. *Task Force Report: Juvenile Delinquency and Youth Crime.* President's Commission on Law Enforcement and Administration of Justice, 1967.
43. *Task Force Report: Narcotics and Drug Abuse.* President's Commission on Law Enforcement and Administration of Justice, 1967.
44. *The Public Looks at Crime and Corrections.* Joint Commission on Correctional Manpower and Training, 1968.
45. Thorwald, Jurgen: *Crime and Science.* New York, HarBrace, 1966.
46. West, D. J.: *The Young Offenders.* New York, Intl Univs Pr, 1967.
47. Winters, J. E.: *Crime and Kids—a Police Approach to the Prevention and Control of Juvenile Delinquency.* Springfield, Thomas, 1959.
48. Witmer, H. and Katensky, R.: *New Perspectives for Research in Juvenile Delinquency.* U.S. Children's Bureau Publication #356, 1956.
49. Wolfgang, Marvin E. and Ferracuti, Franco: *Subculture of Violence.* New York, Pub. by Tavistock B & N, 1967.
50. Wolfgang, M. E.: *Crime and Race.* Institute of Human Relations Press, 1964.

CHAPTER EIGHT

SUICIDE, HOMICIDE,

OR BOTH

SUICIDE

THE AVERAGE CITIZEN VIEWS SUICIDE as being opposite and contradictory to homicide. Psychologically, the two acts are intimately related and the underlying motives intersect in most situations.

Some Clues to Suicide

It has been estimated that approximately 80 percent of suicidal people give some advance warning of their intentions. The difficulty is in having someone sensitive enough to pick up the signal and interpret it correctly. Focusing on the clues to potential suicide is one of the functions of the trained observer.

The clues usually develop in advance of the actual suicide by at least two weeks. These clues are classified in four general categories: verbal, behavioral, situational, and syndromatic.[17]

VERBAL. There can be direct and indirect verbal clues. The direct are actual statements to the effect of an intent to commit suicide, "I have nothing to live for," "If he doesn't come back, I'll kill myself." Indirect verbal clues include such comments as "I'm just a stone around your neck," "You'd be better off without me," "I can't put up with this way of life anymore, I've had it." Other indirect communications presaging suicide attempts include joking and pseudo humor. These might involve laughingly saying, "I think I'll go home and hang myself," or "For two cents I'd blow my brains out."

In general suicidologists have found that any direct or indirect references to suicide should be taken seriously since significant numbers of people who communicate these intentions do follow through on them at some point.

BEHAVIORAL. All suicide attempts are direct behavioral communications of a serious suicide intent. The harmful use of pills, knife, rope or chemicals are direct attempts to communicate a serious problem. Indirect clues involve the sudden making out of a will, giving away prize possessions, or arranging for one's own burial.

SITUATIONAL CLUES. In a crisis situation where the individual is under extreme stress, constituting a kind of psychological emergency, there may be a communication of suicidal intent. This can involve extreme anxiety about hospitalization, surgery, physical illness, or some other feared event.

SYNDROMATIC CLUES. When separate symptoms or clues are put together, a syndrome or picture of suicide intent emerges. Four of the main suicidal syndromes involve depression, disorientation, defiance, and dependency with dissatisfaction.

The suicidal person quickly becomes apathetic, anxious, self-critical and very withdrawn. He may lose his appetite, lose weight rapidly, have difficulty sleeping, lack energy, be lethargic, lose interest in his appearance, his sexual life and other everyday activities. It usually becomes harder for the depressed person to communicate. While deeply depressed, the individual usually lacks the energy to carry out his suicidal wish.

Most suicides related to the depressive syndrome occur after the individual begins to feel better, and has mobilized enough energy to follow through on his self-punitive impulses. Approximately one-third of all suicides appear to involve the depressive syndrome.

The disorientation syndrome involves difficulty in relating to the environment and the real world. There is frequently a feeling of confusion, which may include delusions or hallucinations of voices which tell him to kill or mutilate himself. In the disoriented state, poor reality testing can result from organic brain damage, drug abuse or other toxic conditions as well as severe psychotic disturbances. Clues such as bizarre behavior, fear of death, and confused awareness of the environment are part of this syndrome.

The defiant syndrome involves more direct aggression and hostility. The individual who exhibits this behavior is usually one with a strong need to control his environment. Being more active than passive, he doesn't wait for things to occur, but makes sure that he is the one in control who takes action and causes things to happen. Typically, he manipulates his environment so that his own needs get met. This kind of individual may have a low frustration tolerance and be fairly rigid in his functioning, exhibiting demanding, critical or aggressive behavior to those in authority.

The dependency-dissatisfaction syndrome involves the individual who is extremely dependent on others, but who is extremely hostile and resentful about being dependent. This person can also be depressed and express feelings of guilt and inadequacy. There is a tendency to complain, to use physical symptoms and pains in expressing dissatisfaction with those trying to help them.

Data on Suicides

Suicide cuts across all socioeconomic levels and affects rich, poor and various occupational groups. In Western countries, more men than women commit suicide although more women attempt suicide unsuccessfully than men.

The number of completed suicides in the United States each year is estimated at approximately 40,000 not counting indirect *accidental* forms. The rate has remained stable since 1900 with an average of about 10.7 suicides per 100,000 population. There are approximately ten attempts for every completed suicide totaling about one quarter million people who have tried suicide each year.[1]

Currently in the United States, the professional group with the highest suicide rate are dentists, with psychiatrists being second and physicians in general, third. As for policemen, Niederhoffer[15] reported that from 1950 to 1965 the average suicide rate for New York City was 11.5 while for the New York Police Department the rate was 22.7 per hundred thousand population. When adjusted for variations the NYPD suicide rate was 50 percent above the average for the general population. However, subsequent figures after that year indicated a reduction in suicide rate closer to the average. This was attributed to the increased stability of the NYPD.[18]

In Western countries the frequency of suicide increases with age. Below age fifteen, suicides are very rare with the trend going from 3.6 per hundred-thousand in the 15 to 19 year-old groups to 27.9 per hundred-thousand in the 75 to 84 year-old group. However, in countries such as Japan, the suicide rate for youths is very high and is the most frequent cause of death for people under thirty.

Meanings of Suicidal Behavior

Suicide has to be interpreted according to the society in which it occurs. One culture may produce more suicide susceptible personalities than another. Suicide can be examined in terms of two basic characteristics, intention and outcome. In order to qualify as a suicide, the individual must intend to kill himself and must actually carry it out. In many instances it is difficult to determine the intention of the person, as studies of fatal one-car accidents have pointed out.[11]

It has been clearly demonstrated that in a large percentage of suicidal situations the basic communication is a cry for help.[7] Even though the intent to suicide may be very determined and strong, the individual may have a fantasy or hope of being rescued. In understanding the meaning of suicide, unconscious motivations and impulses also have to be considered. Freud has pointed out that the individual does not usually conceive of his own permanent death.[9] There may be a wish to join a lost loved one or a desire to get even for an injustice or hurt.

At an unconscious level, suicide can be an attempt to strike back and punish the internalized image of a parent, spouse or sibling. If the suicidal individual feels closely identified and intertwined with the loved and hated introject, then suicide may seem to be one way of getting rid of the ambivalent feeling.

Another motive for suicidal behavior may be testing-out of oneself by taking risks or gambling with death. This can involve direct risk-taking such as Russian roulette or less obvious activities which could eventuate in the individual's death. However, most suicides appear to be committed by psychologically disturbed individuals who have felt a severe loss or deprivation. There is often a feeling of helplessness, despair, and a lack of hope.[10]

Individuals who find it difficult to maintain a future orientation, who tend to dwell in the past are often more prone to suicide because of a lack of hope and a lack of direction.

Suicide has also been termed a turning of anger on-the-self. Because of cultural conditioning and taboos against acting-out of hostile behavior, an individual may become angry and feel a murderous rage toward someone close to him but feel guilty about expressing it directly. He may then turn it on himself, feeling worthless and inadequate, and strike at the internalized object of the person who is hated.

In some instances suicide can be seen as an extension of childhood feelings of evoking sympathy and affection from parents. The child who threatens to leave home or run away in order to make parents love him and feel guilt for mistreatment is an example of this pattern. "If you lose me, then you will be sorry and love me more."

Suicide can also be related to environmental circumstances. During times of crisis such as war, flood or other catastrophic events, there seems to be a unifying force because of the externalizing of one's concerns and energies. People are more likely to put aside their own problems and work together to overcome a common obstacle. However, when these crises and threats are no longer available as an external focus, there will likely be an increase in self-preoccupation and feelings of despair.

Another motive for suicide is the attempt to overcome passivity. The suicide act itself represents a rebellious attitude which says, "I can take this positive action and declare to everybody that I am capable." Still another motive is the need for punishment because of guilt feelings and a desire for expiation.

Suicide may be perceived as a kind of rebirth, free of old sins and crimes. Although alcohol is frequently involved in suicidal situations, it is usually not the primary cause. It reduces inner controls and inhibitions so that basic impulses can be more easily acted upon.

Certain individuals are more prone to suicide than others, depending on personality factors. Studies of infants and small children suggest that a history of parental loss in childhood predisposes the individual toward insecurity, lack of confidence and a shaky self-image. In general, suicidal people tend to possess underlying personality damage which renders them less able to tolerate frustrations and disappointment later in life.

In 1938, Karl Menninger classified suicide into several different categories.[14] He indicated that suicide is a very complex act psychologically rather than a simple, isolated event. He described three components in the suicidal act.

First, the act of murder, which is a murder of the self. The first component of the self-murder is the wish to kill, with destructive impulses directed outwardly. The second component is the wish to be killed which is an extreme form of submission, as killing is the extreme form of aggression. This is related to a wish to suffer, to submit to pain because of feelings of conscience and the need for self-punishment. The third component is the wish to die. The conscious wish to die may be a feeling of wanting to get even.

Menninger also discusses various forms of chronic suicide. These involve long-term, self-destructive situations which might include drug addictions, neurotic invalidism, anti-social behavior or psychosis. These can be viewed as a destructive withering away of the individual.

He differentiates chronic suicide from focal suicide in that focal suicide involves a specific self-destructive activity such as a self-mutilation, arranging for unnecessary surgery, having an accident, or even hurting oneself by impotence or frigidity.

His third category of suicides are the organic suicides which involve the development of an actual organic disease or illness which represents the lesser of the evils among the choices of self-destruction. Although it is slow suicide, it provides the needed punishment and allows the individual to remain alive even though his functioning is severely limited.

The Relationship to Homicide

The common link between homicide and suicide is aggressive impulses. Murder may be followed by suicide, and in England approximately one-third of all murders are. Whether the aggression will be directed outward or inward on the self, or both, hinges on the amount of love and hate involved in the significant relationship. Frequently, there is a long, stormy emotional situation before the lethal outburst. There may have been open signs of hostility, jealousy, resentment, and violent temper.

People liable to commit murder-suicide crimes are those with a high level of aggression which may turn against others or against themselves according to circumstances. Their aggression is expressed in personal relationships rather than in criminal acts such as robbery, burglary or assault. In a sample of murderers, it was found that they were unusually prone to suicide attempts. In some respects the murderer group resembled a sample of suicides, including socioeconomic status and sex distribution. They tended to be somewhat younger in age than suicide groups but older than murderer groups.

Among the murderer-suicide population with mental abnormalities, severe depression was the commonest syndrome as it is among plain suicide groups. However, among ordinary murderers with mental disturbances, schizophrenia and paranoid states seem more common. A conclusion of this study was that insane offenders involved in murder-suicide cannot be distinguished from the sane offenders by the method of killing or motive involved.[20]

There were no striking contrasts between the times chosen for murder-suicide and the ordinary murder. In both cases the frequent time was late at night. Murder-suicide by sane persons acting under duress seems very similar to the ordinary suicide situation. Precipitating stressors in both cases are despair, hopelessness, impulsive aggression resulting from a frustrating love affair, or inability to tolerate financial or sexual frustrations.

Suicide Prevention

Suicide prevention involves being able to discern the clues of a suicide attempt and having the courage to take appropriate steps to prevent the suicide from being acted-out. It may involve defying family members, referral for psychiatric assistance, arranging for hospitalization, or whatever other steps seem to be appropriate in a particular situation.

Many people who consciously intend to kill themselves still unconsciously want to be saved. The police officer may be on the scene and may be able to recognize when the suicidal individual is still teetering between his wish to live and his wish to die. By recognizing the clues and taking effective action, he may be preventing the waste of much human potential.

Although the suicidal individual frequently feels helpless and sees no hope for himself, it is because he is so surrounded by his own despair and confusion that he loses his objectivity. Often with a surprisingly small amount of psychological assistance, the person in a suicidal state of mind can be helped to see alternatives he was not aware of. He can learn to look to the future for satisfaction, hope, and pleasure rather than acting on his impulse of the moment which will cut short what could be a worthwhile and satisfying life.

HOMICIDE

Some homicides are justifiable. Those that are not are called murder. In 1960 there were 16,000 criminal homicides in the United States representing a 76 percent increase over the decade, the number one position among Western nations for this crime. The increase in murder along with the increase in other kinds of violent acting-out behavior stimulates fascination with destructive behavior.

Who, What, When, Where

Most killers are not actually psychotic. In three out of four murders the victim and perpetrator knew each other. In 25 percent of the cases they were related to each other. Five out of six killers are men and 60 percent of murderers are Negroes in addition to 55 percent of the victims.

In 1970, 43 percent of the suspects arrested for murder were under twenty-five years of age, and 10 percent under the age of eighteen. About half of all the killings occurred in the South with the murder rate being highest in the big cities. This represents an urban murder rate of 17.5 per hundred-thousand population compared with 6.4 in rural and 3.8 per hundred-thousand in suburban areas. Guns are used in 65 percent of all United States murders whereas 20 percent of the victims are killed by knife, and by poison rarely.

Most killings are impulsive in nature, an emotional explosive acting-out which may have been precipitated by a minor insult or argument over love, sex or money. Many of these murders are done by people who normally tend to be over-conforming, over-controlled, but who break out into extreme violence when provoked enough. In approximately 20 percent of the cases, the murder was done acting in self-defense rather than intending to murder.

In some instances, a murder can be committed as a way of getting killed in return. More slayings occur in the home than outside the home. Men kill more frequently in the street while women kill most often in the kitchen and are killed most often in the bedroom. Private homes are more lethal than public places. Murder is also most likely to happen in the central business area of the city.

People in high homicide areas are frequently employed in lower levels of the occupational structure. They contain about half of the city's unemployed and have a lower educational status. In about 70 percent of the cases the murderer and victim live less than two miles apart with 33 percent living at the same address or within the same block.[21]

Homicides frequently occur during leisure time and are associated with recreational activities. Drinking may be involved, as in the Saturday night drinking spree. It is usually committed against someone where personal feelings are involved, friends, family, acquaintances, neighbors, or companions. Homicide, as well as suicide and sex crimes, is more frequent in the summer months. Weekends and holidays are also more frequent times for murder as is nighttime with 54 percent of the murders taking place between 8 p.m. and 2 a.m.

While suicide tends to steadily increase with age, premeditated and unpremeditated murder increase to about age thirty-five and then decrease. Those who do the killing are younger than the victims on the average. Murderers have their highest rate between twenty and twenty-four years of age, with the second highest rate between thirty-five and twenty-nine. Both Negro and white males have the strongest capability for committing homicide between twenty and twenty-four years of age. Only 9 percent of all murderers were fifty years or older. However, women are more likely to be offenders at later ages than men.[12]

Women have a lower murder rate than men which may be related to the cultural notion that women are more passive. However, this seems to be changing currently along with the emphasis on equality between the sexes and on women's liberation. Female offenders usually kill their husbands, lovers and children. In the Philadelphia study[21] Negro female murderers had a rate 23 times greater than the white female offenders, while the rate for Negro male offenders was 12 times as great as for the white male offenders.

This study also indicated that 64 percent of the perpetrators had previous arrest records and that most of these were offenses against the person with 73 percent having had a record of aggravated assault. The records also involve previous convictions with light sentences and little constructive intervention. This suggests that homicide is a crime built upon previous aggressive acting-out in the form of assault or emotional outbursts.

Passion or Profit—Some Data

Relatively few murders are committed for profit. Most are the result of anger and frustration of people who are either related or acquainted in some way.

The police officer is very concerned about his need to kill a suspect or the possibility of his own death. Wolfgang[21] found that policemen involved in justifiable homicides had victim offenders who were Negroes approximately 6 to 29 times the rate of white offenders among ten cities sampled. The participation of females was negligible.

Usually the victims of these slayings were young with approximately half being under twenty-eight years of age. Most of the victims were killed between 9 P.M. and 9 A.M., with crimes involving resisting arrest and assault with intent to kill the police officer. About two-thirds had previous criminal records and had been sentenced to penal institutions at least once. There was also a history of violent acting-out in most cases. One conclusion reached was that the criminals killed by police officers are usually responsible for their own deaths by their provocative behavior.

The tendency for lower class minority groups to have a disproportionate number of homicides has been connected by some sociologists to the *subculture of violence*. This refers to the social isolation and development of a value system which condones physical violence and aggressiveness starting in childhood and then pervading the whole subculture.[22]

Rather than profit, criminal homicide results from domestic quarrels, jealousy, arguments over money or insult. Most of the victim-offenders were related or had frequent contact. In general victims are assaulted homicidally by members of their own race.

There is a group of murders which have been precipitated by the victim. These commonly occur in mate slayings where alcohol has been involved and where the victim provokes the assault with the clear knowledge that violent acting-out behavior will occur.

In general, homicides are mainly crimes of passion rather than being premeditated or involving psychotic functioning. The proponents of the subculture of violence theory point out that the highest incidence of rapes, aggravated assaults and recidivism also occur among the groups with the highest homicide rates, suggesting that violent behavior is learned early and becomes a way of life for those individuals.[22]

Common Patterns of Violence

Although aggressive impulses are innate in human beings, there are usually defenses developed against direct expression of anger and murderous rage. The kinds of defenses developed are in part shaped by environmental influences. If acting-out and lack of self-control are acceptable behaviors in the environment then this pattern will be learned by the individual in the course of growing up. It becomes internalized as acceptable behavior in the individual's value system.

The paid assassin may or may not be a mentally disturbed individual. He may be murdering for profit or for political zeal. He may feel motivated by what he feels are the highest of goals, saving his country or even the world. Murder may also be precipitated by psychotic level disturbance related to drug taking. The psychotomimetic drugs have been centrally linked to certain ritual and mass murders. In addition there are satanists whose philosophy of life contains the notion of absolution or influencing of supernatural powers by sacrifice. This atavistic practice involves a victim who is killed as an offering.

A percentage of murders are perpetrated by severely emotionally disturbed individuals who may or may not be legally insane. A few of the more bizarre murders involve cannibalism, dismemberment and sadistic mutilation.

In England, 30 percent or more of murderers are found insane compared with less than 5 percent in the United States.[13]

HOMICIDE PREVENTION

Homicide, like other human disturbances, seems to be related to environmental as well as personality and family variables. A program of prevention must have impact on the long-range sociological factors as well as on those affecting the individual's internal controls. The connection of early childhood development and later criminal behavior involving violent acting-out have been well-documented. Providing adequate parenting and satisfaction of basic needs during childhood is an important need in the prevention area.

It will also be necessary to restructure our rehabilitation programs for those already identified as violence prone. Because the data suggests that a majority of murderers have been identified by previous contacts with the law, or by their pattern of behavior, it is necessary that there be effective treatment programs available to which these individuals can be referred. In too many instances persons identified as dangerous to themselves or to others are released without adequate attention, culminating in a later tragedy.

From the police officer's point of view, threats to kill, like threats of suicide, should be taken seriously. In many instances the threats are carried out. Rather than *kissing off* a threat because no crime has been committed as yet, the police need to develop some techniques of intervening as they do in attempt suicide situations. Supporting legislation may be necessary for this to work.

The paranoid individual who feels persecuted may attempt to get help from some recognized agency, and if he is not handled properly, may decide to take action himself. Officers encountering persons with delusions of persecution, with anger and a need to defend against imagined assault, should be alert to the possibility of homicidal acting-out.

BIBLIOGRAPHY

1. Anderson, Dorothy B. and McClean, Lenora: *Identifying Suicide Potential*. Behavioral Publications, 1971.
2. Arons, Harry: *Hypnosis in Criminal Investigation*. Springfield, Thomas, 1967.
3. Arther, Richard: *The Scientific Investigator*. Springfield, Thomas, 1965.
4. Boudaris, James: Homicide and the family. *Journal of Marriage and the Family*, November, 1971, pp. 667-676.
5. Camps, F. E.: *The Investigation of Murder*. Michael Joseph, 1966.
6. Farber, Maurice: *Theory of Suicide*. New York, Funk & W, 1968.
7. Farberow, N. and Shneidman, E.: *The Cry for Help*. New York, McGraw, 1961.
8. Finch, Stuart and Poznanski, Elva: *Adolescent Suicide*. Springfield, Thomas, 1971.
9. Freud, Sigmund: Mourning and melancholia, in *Collected Papers*, Vol. IV, London, Hogarth, 1949.
10. Gaylin, Willard: *The Meaning of Despair*. New York, Science, 1968.
11. Litman, Robert and Tabachnick, Norman: Fatal one-car accidents, *Psychoanalytic Quarterly*, 1967, 36, pp. 248-259.
12. Macdonald, John M.: *The Murderer and His Victim*. Springfield, Thomas, 1961.
13. Macdonald, J. M.: *Homicidal Threats*. Springfield, Thomas, 1968.
14. Menninger, Karl: *Man Against Himself*. New York, HarBrace J, 1938.
15. Niederhoffer, Arthur: *Behind the Shield: The Police in Urban Society*. Garden City, Doubleday, 1967.
16. Pretzel, Paul: *Understanding and Counseling the Suicidal Person*. Nashville, Abingdon, 1972.
17. Shneidman, Edwin: Preventing suicide. *American Journal of Nursing*, May, 1965.
18. Shneidman, Edwin: *Essays in Self-Destruction*. New York, Science, 1967.
19. *Suicidal Behavior and Law Enforcement*. Law Enforcement Study Center, Washington University, 1970.
20. West, D. J.: *Murder Followed by Suicide*. London, Heinemann, 1965.
21. Wolfgang, Marvin E.: *Patterns in Criminal Homicide*. Philadelphia, U of Pa Pr, 1958.
22. Wolfgang, Marvin E. and Ferracuti, Franco: *Subculture of Violence*. New York, Pub. by Tavistock B. & N., 1967.

CHAPTER NINE

PSYCHOLOGY APPLIED TO

FIELD SITUATIONS

ALTHOUGH HE MAY NOT consciously be aware of it, the police officer is daily using psychology in his interactions with people on the street. Because he deals primarily with people problems, the police officer of necessity must develop and utilize his faculties as a trained observer, and in a very practical fashion apply basic psychologic know-how in doing his job effectively and economically.

ON BEING PROVOKED AND CHALLENGED

The policeman is the symbol of authority and represents the establishment and the status quo. Easily identified by his uniform and the emblems of power that he carries, the policeman is a ready-made target for many citizens who have unresolved conflicts about dependency and authority.

His visibility and presence as the authority symbol combined with the unconscious mixed feelings of love and hate that people have, motivate some citizens in the community to react with anger, provocation or seductiveness even though they do not know the policeman personally. A wide range of stereotyped reactions exhibited toward the police officer must be examined as almost automatic responses toward a symbol of authority rather than realistic feelings toward the individual man inside the uniform.

One of the common problems that many male and female suspects and citizens have is that of uncertain identification, with insecurity, lack of confidence, and a strong and sometimes overwhelming need to prove oneself. This is encountered by policemen daily when a provocative male suspect challenges the officer in an attempt to get the authority symbol into a face-to-face confrontation and fight. The reason is that the hostile male suspect is basically unsure about his masculinity and his adequacy as a male.

Because of his insecurity and his anxiety, he attempts to prove himself by challenge in much the same way that children play *knock the chip off my shoulder.* The amount of provocation and hostility is often an index of the severity of the unresolved identification problem.

The police officer, being a professional and being secure about his own identity, knows that the challenge is not his problem as long as it remains on a verbal level. He asks himself the question *Whose problem is it?* The answer is, *It is the suspect's problem.* Therefore, rather than getting manipulated into a knock-down, drag-out fight with an insecure suspect, the professional officer verbally reassures the individual with a comment such as "I know you're a man. You don't have to prove it." He then goes about his business quietly and efficiently.

Of course, there are insecure individuals with very poor self-control and if the assault becomes physical rather than verbal, the officer contains the suspect with the minimum necessary force. It is usually easier to talk a suspect into jail than to fight him in.

Young policemen who tend to get into many altercations and physical confrontations with suspects and citizens need to take a careful look at themselves. Exaggerated feelings of insecurity combined with self-doubt about manliness will interfere with the process of becoming a professional officer.

The professional maintains a sense of humor, and yet knows how to be firm without being badge-heavy when the situation calls for it. He has an air of authority, based on knowledge of his job and a sense of competence. He is not authoritarian, avoiding a superior attitude or a tendency to look down on other people. He treats even criminals as human.

COMMUNICATING WITH PEOPLE

Communications make human interactions possible. A variety of communications tools are extremely important to the professional person including the police officer.

Every person needs to feel important. If we respect this need in communicating with people either verbally or non-verbally, we will improve communication. However, when this basic need is disregarded, a lot of words may be used but the intended message does not get across. Words are very important tools of the trade. In addition, the tone of voice and manner of speaking can either reinforce what is said or negate it completely.

By speaking courteously and with consideration for the other person, we set the tone for the kind of transaction we expect to have. Most people respond to these cues and expectations. In respecting other people we are also indicating that we respect ourselves. Looking down on others or treating them as inferiors reveals our own unconscious feelings of inadequacy.

Many of the problems police officers commonly experience in communicating with people involve very simple kinds of behavior. Profanity, name-calling, references to ethnic origin, physical appearance, skin color, sex, or becoming overly familiar with someone all communicate one's own problems. A rule of thumb is not to use someone's first name unless you expect yours to be used as well. Because teenagers are very sensitive to being patronized, they should be approached and talked to as young ladies and men rather than as children or *punks*.

In addition to words there are other non-verbal communications which affect every transaction. If there is a disparity between what is being said and the behavior of the speaker, the actions will prevail rather than the words. Non-verbal communications may involve pushing someone, turning your back on the person while he is talking, or angrily stabbing him in the chest with a finger. These communications convey anger, disrespect and lack of self-control. They tend to arouse reciprocal feelings.

One of the most difficult tasks to learn in communicating adequately is the art of listening. The trained professional learns to listen carefully in assessing situations. By listening rather than talking, he allows the citizen or suspect to vent some of his pent-up feelings, lower his tension level and reduce his stress and anxiety.

As he gets his feelings off his chest, the person feels he is no longer alone, someone is sharing his problem. Consequently, he may begin to feel less depressed and angry by tuning-in on the tone of voice and bodily mannerisms of the speaker, the experienced officer gets additional information about the person which enables him to handle the situation with greater incisiveness and dispatch.

One of the inexperienced officer's biggest communication problems results from oversight, being in a hurry, and having a poor attitude. It is important to explain police actions to people. We all have a right to know why something is being done to us. The professional policeman accepts this as legitimate and necessary and takes the extra few seconds to explain to the individual why he is being stopped, searched, handcuffed or questioned. This lets the person know that the transaction is a professional one and not personal.

The professional is also aware that physically touching someone unannounced can result in an explosive situation. Being touched by an authority figure may be interpreted as an attack and violent reactions may result. The officer is aware of the sensitive nature of this kind of interaction, and where he has to pat someone down or otherwise touch, he gives a brief explanation in advance, which puts the transaction on a professional basis.

The experienced officer realizes that an explanation is neither a pampering of the citizen nor a sign of weakness on his part. It merely represents the professional approach in getting the job done in the easiest, least stressful way.

The words can be right but if the manner is overly serious or rigid the communication can come across differently. Overseriousness is an occupational hazard that results in part from defending against personal involvement and tragic human events. However, curtness and coldness in communicating with people frequently leads to misunderstanding. A smile or kind word reminds the citizen that the policeman is really a human being and not solely a rigid authority figure lacking in empathy or understanding.

FAMILY DISPUTES

As much as 40 percent of the average patrolman's time may be spent in handling family disputes. Of necessity, the police officer becomes knowledgeable and comfortable in dealing with these situations as a regular part of his job. Family disputes are potentially explosive and dangerous.

In the past, more police officers have been killed and injured in family dispute interventions than in robbery and burglary situations. However, the experience of the Family Crisis Intervention Unit in New York,[1, 2] has shown that with careful training, motivation and aptitude on the part of the officers, injury can be avoided.

Handling family disputes can be seen as having three main phases. The first phase is the initial intervention. The second consists of a combination of defusing and assessment, and the third phase involves resolution and/or referral.

The initial intervention is critical. Very often the manner of approach of the officers has a lot to do with the outcome of the transaction. A few ground rules that have been developed are: (1) stay calm, (2) don't threaten, (3) don't take sides, (4) don't challenge a man's masculinity, (5) don't degrade a woman's feminity, (6) give verbal escape routes to help the people save face.

In initial intervention it is always desirable to take sufficient time to get any available background information and to approach the situation slowly and thoughtfully rather than rushing in impulsively. Kicking in doors and accepting the challenge of a provocative suspect very often lead to physical violence.

In defusing and assessing the situation, listening is very important. Listening uncritically without taking sides, allowing the person to blow off steam and get rid of some of the tension and hostility can be a very helpful defuser in a potentially explosive situation.

In assessing the seriousness and chronicity of the family dispute, one can ask non-threatening questions about the frequency of the family disputes, how long it has existed, what precipitated it, and what are the underlying unconscious motives for the family dispute as well as the more obvious ones. Are there emotional disturbances that require professional help?

Although many police officers are very good practical psychologists, it is not appropriate for them to get involved in actual therapy. In these cases, the most helpful thing that can be done is to make an appropriate referral to a community agency. In order to do this the officer must be knowledgeable about the resources in his community, including hours, costs and staff.

He should also be willing to help get people connected by making the initial phone call. The officer should proceed realizing that a mishandled or poorly handled family dispute can lead to a more serious recurrence and the possibility of a fellow police officer getting injured subsequently. Adequately handling a family dispute is as important as any other police technique.

Where radio cars are assigned to a specific territory, teams should keep index cards on family dispute situations so that they become familiar with families having chronic problems. This will help in diagnosing which situations are potentially dangerous to the officer or to a family member, and aid in the assessment and resolution of the current conflict.

Some of the major causes of family disputes involve money, sex, parent-child conflicts, alcoholism and depression or fear. The officer should feel comfortable in discussing with the family disputants material related to any of these areas and be prepared to make some practical suggestions about how the individuals may resolve their conflict.

In many family disputes the basic problem is one of ego injury. One partner criticizes, attacks or puts-down the other, causing a hostile, aggressive reaction with a desire to retaliate. By focusing on the positive traits of each of the individuals and by giving ego support, such as acknowledging a male's masculinity and adequacy and a female's feminity in a non-manipulative way, the officer can help restore some of the lost esteem that may be at the botton of a family fight.

One of the standard procedures that has been developed for intervening in family disputes involves having the officers go in together, separating the disputants, with one officer going with each into a separate room. Next, allowing the person to talk and explain the situation, asking questions to clarify, having the officers switch disputants to check out stories and get a better evaluation of the total situation, finding out about previous history of disputes within the family, and then finally bringing the couple together to tell their stories to each other, but permitting only one to talk at a time.

The officers can then point out discrepancies, contradictions, or common feelings, and get a reaction from the two disputants after making suggestions. Finally, they should be asked what they plan to do about the situation. If the response seems realistic and agreeable, the conflict can be resolved at that point. However, if it seems desirable and necessary, a referral should be made. This may involve *selling* the referral and the advantages of getting outside help.

Finally, if the radio car plan allows it, the officers should give their names and phone number and indicate that they will be available for further consultation should the conflict erupt at some future time.

Intervening in a crisis situation carries the potential for a higher level of adjustment if the conflict is successfully resolved and some of the basic issues are understood by the disputants. The reason is that the strong emotional feelings involved in the dispute allow the previously established balance in the relationship to be upset. Where the new balance will be is a function of many variables including what kinds of inputs are provided during the intervention.

The counseling process involves certain stages which should be understood by the police officer. The first task in counseling is to establish rapport. This is best done by communicating an attitude of equal adults, rather than threatening, talking down to, or treating the individuals as children or inferiors.

Establishing an informal atmosphere is helpful. By removing the hat, sitting down, sharing a cup of coffee and similar techniques, an air of relaxation can be fostered. This helps change the threatening authority figure into a human being who may really be interested in their problems.

The second task in counseling is to listen carefully and nonjudgmentally. By merely listening, several things are accomplished. First, listening gives ego support to the individual who then no longer feels alone with the weight of the world on his shoulders, since someone else is now sharing the burden. Second, it allows the individual to ventilate and get things off his chest. This reduces the tension, anxiety and anger considerably. Finally, by being a quiet sounding board, the officer allows the individual to listen to himself without interruption and gain some insight into his feelings and ideas.

Another task of the counselor is to reflect and clarify feelings. This can best be done by asking open-ended questions to elicit more information. This is communicated as a friendly desire to know more about the situation rather than a third-degree type of interrogation. Open-ended questions cannot be answered by a simple *yes* or *no*, but require fuller expression and explanation.

After sufficient information is gathered to provide an overview of the situation, the officers can give a reflective summary. This is simply their understanding of the situation, how they see it in terms of the precipitating factors.

The final task in the counseling process is to discuss with the disputants, alternative approaches to the problem in order to arrive at some resolution. This may involve further discussion on their part, or it may involve seeking some outside counseling help from an agency or private practitioner.

Young policemen sometimes feel at a disadvantage and ill-at-ease when attempting to intervene in a family dispute involving older people who have obviously been married a long time. However, this is a personal reaction in which he is allowing his youth and personal feelings to intrude into the situation. The officer is a professional because of his expertise regardless of his age, his own marital status or personal problems. He is aware that the problems under discussion are not his, and his role is as a mediator and helper in problem resolution.

The officer should consider some of the unconscious motives behind family disputes. This may involve a chronic wife-beating situation where the husband gets satisfaction by being brutal and sadistic towards his wife, and the wife unconsciously gets pleasure out of being beaten by her husband, although consciously she may complain about it.

This may be reflected in the common Saturday night drinking, wife-beating spree where the wife will complain and want the husband arrested after being severely beaten. However, she will soon go down to have him released from jail so that they can resume their sado-masochistic relationship.

HANDLING MENTALLY ILL

Currently, the police officer is the only 24-hour, 7-days-a-week professional available to handle psychiatric emergencies in the community. Therefore, he is an important resource in the area of mental health.

Although he may not have extensive formal training in psychiatry, the policeman's frequent exposure to emergency situations helps make him knowledgeable and experienced in handling psychiatric problems, especially cases involving violence. In this connection, mental health experts have sometimes requested training and assistance from police officers in dealing with agitated or aggressive patients in the community.

Mental illness ranges from the helplessness of the feeble, sick, injured, senile, or amnesic person, to the nuisance type with mildly annoying acting-out in public, to the violently aggressive individual. In a great many instances, the hostile, acting-out individual is more self-punitive than injurious to others. However, the line between self-injury and injury to others is sometimes shaky.

Dealing with mental illness of any type requires skill, patience and understanding on the part of the police officer. The majority of mentally ill individuals are withdrawn, uncommunicative and passive rather than hostile, angry or aggressive. They frequently feel relief when there is someone to help who can exert external control, reducing the fear and anxiety generated by insufficient inner controls.

There are some basic guidelines which can be of help to police officers in assisting mentally ill persons.[21]

1. Get as much background information about the situation as possible. Take all the time that's necessary rather than rushing in impulsively. In most cases a slow and leisurely pace is more comforting to the patient and safer for the officer. Talking with witnesses, family, friends, will help to provide a more realistic assessment of the situation and avoid unnecessary danger.

2. When in doubt call for assistance. This can represent security to the patient and motivate him to respond more agreeably. Calling for assistance rather than fighting a mentally ill person is more professional and intelligent.

3. Explain to the person what you are going to do before you

do it. Don't lie to him or talk as if he can't possibly understand what's going on or that he doesn't need to know what's going on. Communicate with the individual as if he is rational and normal and an ally in your attempt to assist him.

4. If there is cursing, verbal abuse or anger maintain objectivity and understanding and recognize that it is directed to you as an authority symbol and not to you as a person.

5. Avoid threatening, hitting or using physical force except in extreme cases. Usually mentally ill individuals are compliant and agreeable if they are given adequate reassurance and the policeman communicates that he is a friend who will help rather than threaten the individual's already shaky stability.

With seriously disturbed people who constitute a threat to themselves or to others or are incapable of self-care, involuntary commitment to a mental health facility may be indicated. This can be done either directly on the police officer's petition to the hospital doctor or through the special mental health detail if the department has one. States vary in their mental health laws, with California having a 72-hour commitment provision for severely mentally ill individuals.

The Los Angeles Police Department has a special hospital detail stationed at the Central Receiving Hospital whose function is to give field officers advice, evaluate particular situations involving mentally ill individuals and to arrange for hospitalization when indicated. These officers use two checklists in making judgments.

The first is called Symptoms Indicating Hospitalization and includes (1) pronounced depression or agitation, (2) pronounced paranoia or paranoid trends, (3) pyromaniac tendencies, (4) destructive acting-out behavior, (5) hallucinations or delusions with acting-out, (6) complete loss of contact with reality not due to organic brain damage.

The second list is called Symptoms Not Indicating Hospitalization and includes (1) stroke, (2) physical infirmities, (3) moderate loss of memory, (4) childishness, (5) irritability or restlessness, (6) careless toilet habits, (7) feeding habits, (8) occasional periods of mild depression, (9) moderate confusion.

The experience of the hospital detail indicates that although these officers have limited academic training, their constant involvement in metnally ill cases with resultant practical experience makes them a tremendous aid to the field policeman who is dealing with a complex mentally ill case and needs some consultation.

BATTERED AND ABUSED CHILDREN

The two main types of parental mistreatment of children are abuse and neglect. Abuse is the committing of an act which harms the child physically and psychologically. It has been estimated that child abuse is the leading cause of death of children under five years of age.

Although it is difficult to fix the actual number of child abuse situations from the official reporting figures, a nationwide survey estimated the actual incidence of a variety of types of abuse in 1965 to be somewhere between two and four million cases. Boys outnumber girls among those abused under twelve while females predominate subsequent to that age.

One study indicated that 75 percent of the reported victims were over two years-old and almost half were over six years of age. Nearly one-fifth were teenagers, with the age distribution being similar for all ethnic groups. Over 60 percent of the children reported had a history of prior abuse. Education and occupational levels of the parents involved were much lower than in the general population.

In approximately half of the cases, a mother or stepmother was the perpetrator, while in about 40 percent, a father. As a group, 70 percent of the children were abused by a biological parent, 14 percent by a stepparent, less than 1 percent by an adoptive parent, 2 percent by a foster parent, 1 percent by a sibling, about 4 percent by other relatives, and 7 percent by an unrelated caretaker. The perpetrators of the child abuse had little education and clustered at low socioeconomic levels.[16]

Many more injuries were likely to be inflicted by perpetrators under twenty-five years of age than by older suspects. Those with previous juvenile court contacts or foster care other than parents are likely to have inflicted serious injuries. More serious or fatal injuries were more likely in families where the annual income was under $3,500.

Approximately 87 percent of the cases involved social welfare agencies and 46 percent were court involved while 53 percent had involved the police at some point. Due to the abuse incidents approximately 46 percent of the children were placed outside the home. In about 17 percent of the incidents the suspected perpetrators were indicted. Detentions resulted in approximately 13 percent of the cases and a jail term in 7 percent.

Approximately one thousand abused or neglected child cases are reported annually to Los Angeles County police agencies. Over one-half of the children are under six years of age, and of these, 20 percent are less than three years-old. Every year the county child medical examiner attributes approximately thirty deaths to deliberately inflicted injuries or starvation.[45]

A review of the incidence of child abuse allows a breakdown of categories of underlying factors.[11] These factors are: psychological rejection, angry and uncontrolled disciplinary response, male baby sitter abuse, personality deviance and reality stress, child originated abuse, female baby sitter abuse, and caretaker quarrel.

Paralleling statistical data on deviance among social groups, perpetrators of child abuse tend to be in a lower socioeconomic group financially. The poor tend to express aggressive impulses in a direct and less inhibited fashion by action, while middle class parents tend to use verbal direction and psychological approaches in disciplining children.

The perpetrators of child abuse commonly have emotional problems involving identity crises, and dependency conflict. There are often unrealistic parental demands for performance on the part of the child before the capability is present. This is manifest in severe criticism of the child, anger and rage resulting when the high expectations are not met. In addition, there is a disregard of the child as a separate individual with needs of his own at his particular level of development.

The abusing parent tends to be self-oriented, concerned largely with his own needs rather than with the child's. A large proportion of child abusers have a history of deprivation themselves as children. This has probably contributed to emotional insecurity and lack of basic trust.

In many cases the attack is usually made by one parent with

the other parent often covering up. The child abuser is not especially sociopathic in his personality structure but has severe emotional disturbances. Often the infant is treated as if he were an adult who comprehends and can perform to the parent's expectations.

Frequently the child abusing parent feels insecure, unloved and expects the child to provide reassurance and support. There is a tendency to reverse roles, with the child expected to play the part of the reassuring parent who will protect and give. Because of strong dependency needs and identity conflict, the abusing parent often resents the helplessness of the infant and views the infant as demanding and unreasonable. This leads to frustration and an attack on the child in an attempt to reduce the anger and anxiety.

On an unconscious level the child can represent an image of the parent's bad self, a hated or denying parent, or a frustrating demander of attention and care. Hostile, aggressive acting-out then follows with the child being attacked as the symbol of the disliked image.

Case histories of abusing parents tend to reveal that child abusers have themselves been deprived in their early family environment and tend to unconsciously recreate with their own children the original early family situation. Parents who were beaten as a child have a tendency to beat their own children excessively.

What effect does child abuse have on the child? Overly aggressive abuse by the parent may create a strong sense of guilt which can persist throughout life. This can be manifested later in depression, self-punitive tendencies, and strong feelings of insecurity and unreality.

In addition to parents, child abusers include siblings, baby sitters, other relatives and strangers. The child itself can contribute to being abused by being hyperactive, having an inordinate need for attention, being different from the expectations of the caretaker or merely by having needs at a time when the caretaker is already burdened by external stresses which then causes an overload resulting in rage, anger, and hostile explosive acting-out.

Numerous studies by developmental psychologists emphasize the importance of the earliest years of life in personality growth and in developing a sense of security in the individual. The first year of life in particular is an extremely crucial foundation.[41] In this regard, a child cannot be spoiled during the first year. The parent who is able to focus on the infant's needs rather than his own can provide the necessary mothering, affection and positive emotional regard that helps to insure emotional stability and good health later on.

The police officer is in a unique position as a case finder in situations of child abuse. Very often there is a tendency to react with outrage and anger toward the child abuser. However, the officer should keep in mind that the legal recognition of child abuse is a relatively recent development.

For many years the societal ethic of *sparing the rod and spoiling the child* made physical punishment synonymous with discipline. Today, statutes have delineated that a parent has a reasonable right to control and discipline over a child, but that the state has a protective role and is required to intervene when discipline becomes abuse. Abuse can be psychological and not leave physical marks, but can be even more harmful than some forms of physical punishment.

The policeman not only performs a service for the child by protecting it from further abuse, but also assists the parents to learn better ways of handling their emotions by making appropriate referrals to agencies who specialize in working with child abusers. In a small percentage of extreme cases it may be necessary to remove the child from the home situation because of the imminent danger to life and security.

GROUPS, CROWDS AND RIOTS

Man is basically a social animal with a need to interact and relate to others. He is normally affected by group influences. A set of factors operates in group psychology that can affect the law enforcement officer as well as those in the group.

People group together for a variety of reasons. It is necessary to distinguish what the purpose of the group is in determining an effective approach to a group problem. Two of the main characteristics of group psychology are, the tendency of the individual to identify with the group and to some degree lose his own identity, and the sharing of guilt feelings among members of the group thus reducing individual responsibility.

A large group of people can be a crowd, but there are different types of crowds depending on the motivation for assembling. Two main kinds of crowds are the noncohesive, temporary collection of people such as those looking at an interesting display in a store window, and the cohesive crowd which has some common interest and emotional identification.

There are crowds at political affairs, sporting events, speeches, parades and other events where there is a shared interest. The fact of sharing tends to unite the crowd with the likelihood that group psychology will play an important part in the crowd's behavior. The cohesive crowd can range from the group of conventioneers to the hostile or angry gathering which threatens and verbalizes against the police.

The significant difference between crowds and mobs is that crowds are leaderless and unorganized while mobs are not. Members of a mob are intentionally stimulated, excited and have strongly identified with the group and leaders, thus being subject to easy arousal and acting-out.

Because the individuals in a mob lose their individual identity, become very excited emotionally and have their guilt feelings distributed among large numbers of other people, the behavior of the mob is irrational and potentially violent. The reinforcing interactions of the mob heightens emotional feelings, excitement and need for satisfaction. Often this involves a scapegoat as a symbol of the mob's frustration and anger, and violent acting-out as a way of reducing the intense pent-up feelings.

As a neutral keeper of the peace, the policeman must balance the demonstrators' rights to express ideas and feelings against the rights of other citizens not to be injured or infringed upon. This requires the policeman to remain psychologically aloof from any demonstration.

The concept of an *acceptable level of disruption* has been proposed[43] with the basic notion that any large gathering or demonstration will be disruptive to some degree and the problem is to decide what level of disruption is acceptable in that particular community.

The possibility of panic in a large gathering or mob is an important consideration for law enforcement officers. Panic is extremely contagious and irrational, and represents escape behavior from a dangerous or life-threatening fear.

People in panic usually perceive an imminent threat, feeling partially entrapped and having difficulty escaping from the area. In addition, there is a communications failure within the group causing an intensification of the panic feeling. In preventing panic in crowds, it is important to keep people informed by maintaining communication and by assuring numerous escape routes in the area.[6]

Campus demonstrations and disturbances have been popular and frequent over the past few years. Some of the conclusions resulting from a study of campus disturbances suggest that major protests are twice as likely to occur at private rather than public universities, that the larger institutions are more likely to experience violent or disruptive protests, and that the more selective the university the more likely it will experience a violent protest.

Some of the underlying factors that have been related to campus disturbances are conflict between generations, the feeling of youth of being on the outside of the establishment, archaic educational practices, the breakdown in the respect for authority and also the nation that campus disturbances reflect problems of a larger society.[5]

Riots usually evolve over a long period of time and one of the key ingredients is the hostile belief system.[38] This is a value system which contains many negative, angry and resentful beliefs, frequently regarding the police. Speigel[39] outlines four stages within the riot process.

Phase one involves a precipitating incident. This is a triggering event which usually tends to reinforce some previous hostile beliefs. It may be the arrest of a drunk driver or another type of police-citizen contact which can be used to confirm pre-existing hostile feelings and beliefs.

Phase two involves a street confrontation where agitators begin haranguing a crowd and pushing for violent behavior. This is a crucial stage which can have two outcomes, a spontaneous dissipation or an escalation into an explosive situation. One suggestion is to have known political figures appear and participate at this stage in helping to cool the situation. The absence of high-level concern may suggest uncaring and calloused feelings about the mob's imagined wrongs and needs.

Phase three is the Roman holiday stage with younger people taking over. Action begins with the throwing of bricks, rocks, bottles, breaking windows and lashing out at passing automobiles, with younger children joining in the fun. The carnival atmosphere of phase three involves the taking over of an area and being *king for a day.*

Phase four which occurs seldom is the siege where extreme polarization and lack of communication have resulted in a community war, with firebombing, sniping and other violence occurring, until finally the energy runs down and the conflict grinds to a halt. The aftermath of the riot can be very important in that constructive action may result and a new level of equilibrium can be reached, or the ground work can be set for future riot actions by a denial of problems and return to the status quo.

It has been suggested that humor can be an effective tool in crowd and mob control.[7] The dynamic is that hostility may be discharged through humor. Some of the factors that are relevant to reduction of public tensions are, recognition of the crowd's need to let off steam, patience on the part of the crowd control forces, continuous efforts to maintain the *light touch,* use of music, announcements made of ball scores or other events of interest, and humor directed at the control forces in the form of incongruity. An example might be suggesting that chairs be brought in so that the policemen might relax.

> The presence of police in any great number will almost inevitably arouse feelings of threat, hostility, and fear of arrest and injury. Insofar as these fears are insubstantial fantasies and do not accurately reflect the police attitudes or behavior in the discharge of their duty, these sentiments are destructive of good police work and public order. Means to discharge any gratuitous hostility and fear would be most constructive.[7]

Whenever humor is used in a crowd situation, it should be directed toward control rather than toward any issues political or otherwise that would involve a confrontation. Antagonists should not be ridiculed and whenever possible the humor should be directed toward the police themselves. Humor tends to be contagious and may snowball.

Momboisse[24] discusses some of the psychological influences at work in agitating group behavior. These factors include the novelty of joining a group demonstration which is different from the routine and daily life style. Another factor is suggestion. People in crowds tend to be more suggestible and more easily led than otherwise.

Contagion is another factor which results from emotional stimulation and heightening of feeling by sharing the reactions of others in the crowd. This can also lead the individual to identify with the aggressor. Imitation is also a factor in that the individual wants to do what others are doing in order to conform and get peer group approval. Anonymity is also important. As personal identity is merged with that of the crowd, group psychology takes over and guilt feelings get dissipated enabling the individual to do things in a crowd that he would never think of doing alone.

Another variable is the chance to release suppressed and repressed desires and impulses. Mob behavior is the perfect vehicle for a kind of cathartic acting-out. Giving vent to hidden impulses as part of the mob's emotional reactivity allows the individual to act-out more freely. There is also an enhanced sense of power in being part of an acting-out hostile mob. If the individual has previously felt powerless and helpless, the mob action can be exhilarating in permitting things that are not ordinarily possible.

Finally, defensive righteousness evolves as a way of rationally using whatever behavior occurs in the mob. It boils down to "How can I be blamed if everybody else was doing the same thing? We must have been right."

Perhaps one of the strongest underlying motives for acting-out in mob behavior is power. From the pecking order of chickens in the barnyard to the complex hierarchies of governments and formal organizations, the acquisition of power is extremely important. The use of mobs for temporarily acquiring and wielding power is a strong psychological determinant in the evolution of riots.

INJURIES, MUTILATION AND DEAD BODIES

For new policemen, medical students and others, blood, mayhem and death can be traumatic. The police officer rapidly becomes conditioned to gory smashups on the freeway, odoriferous corpses, sliced or mutilated people, and battered children. Like the medical student, over time he adapts by using a variety of defense mechanisms.

Physical injuries are not only painful in themselves but can also be a psychological threat in that they are a blow to one's narcissism. An injury may force the anxiety-provoking realization that one is not omnipotent. In the normal course of growing up, children develop a concept of self which includes a *body ego*. This is the bodily representation of self exemplified in external appearance, build, size, imagined beauty or toughness and other physical attributes.

Over the years, body integrity, health and illness, hurt and loss are closely related to one's sense-of-self, to being loved or unloved, and to one's need for punishment.

Illness and injuries often cause regression to a childlike feeling of helplessness with increased need for reassurance, attention and affection. Some individuals consciously or unconsciously utilize illness or injury as a way of getting the attention and affection they feel they can't get otherwise.

However, mutilation, or loss of body parts is much more anxiety producing because it not only affects self-image, but also the sense of loss and adequacy as maintained in the body ego. The strong need to maintain physical integrity is seen in the phenomenon of phantom limb. Although an arm or leg has been amputated, sensations are still felt in the missing part. If as if it were still there. This is an attempt to maintain the body ego in phantasy.

In both sexes, the sensitivity and anxiety about mutilation unconsciously centers around genital mutilation and around bodily parts which symbolically are related to the genitals. These include eyes, teeth, tongue and fingers.

Transactions involving dead bodies arouse additional emotions and anxieties. In childhood, separation anxiety results from a fear of being removed from a needed parent who represents security and strength. As the child grows, this anxiety generalizes to other related situations which all involve possible loss. Initially the loss feared was external, involving a secure environment. Over time, it gets internalized so that the anxiety over fear of loss is related to loss of self-control, loss of love, or loss of self-esteem.

The child has no real concept of death. It represents a going away, a trip rather than a finality, so that fears and anxieties about death usually emerge at a later developmental age. To a small child, body and self are indistinguishable. Death and burial may be interpreted to mean that the individual is living beneath the ground.

The adult comes to accept the fact, that with death the self ceases to exist and the body becomes a mass of decaying cells. In this connection, absence or presence of brain function is used medically to determine if life remains. The mind apparently represents the essence of humanness.

Because police work is stressful and dangerous, with the possibility of injury, mutilation or death being real, the man in police work needs to come to terms with these fears and anxieties.

HIGH SPEED PURSUITS

Much research has been done in the area of highway accidents, driving skills and traffic problems. It has been shown that age, sex and judgment are important factors, as is intelligence. Accidents are highest with male drivers under age twenty-four. Female drivers tend to be less accident prone, although at age thirty the difference levels off. The accident rate of trained drivers is approximately one-half that of untrained drivers according to the American Automobile Association.

High speed pursuits are high stress, high risk operations for police officers. Traditionally and psychologically the pursuit represents the essence of the policeman-suspect game. The officer's job is to apprehend the lawbreaker, while the suspect attempts to elude and escape thus frsutrating the authority figure. In a high speed pursuit situation several factors begin operating that increase the probability of emotional reactions and the clouding of judgment and decision-making.

In every stress situation certain physiological reactions occur in human beings. These include increased respiration, heart rate, blood pressure, adrenalin secretion, discharge of corpuscles from the spleen and reserve sugar from the liver. These physiological operations enable the individual to become aroused, reach a state of readiness for possible danger and to adapt to the stress situation.

As part of the arousal mechanism, the individual becomes slightly tense, keyed up, anxious, with all senses operating with increased receptivity. Because these physiological mechanisms come under the control of the autonomic nervous system, they are essentially automatic and minimally controllable. Recent research has indicated, however, that some autonomic physiological operations can be influenced by conscious control techniques.[35] A problem arises when the physiologically aroused individual gets carried away by his emotional state because of underlying psychological factors.

Important psychological variables affecting the police officer under stress consist of background and situational factors. Background variables are those associated with the individual's personality, pre-existing value system and life style. Situational factors are those involved in the stress incident itself.

Emotional instability in the person's personality structure, and temporary maladjustments and disturbances in his personal life tend to lower his resistance to stress. Overall physical condition is also an important factor as well as fatigue or illness. The reactions and judgments of individuals in a stress situation depend on the interaction of two traits which can be called self-confidence and despair.

Each individual maintains a balance between confidence and despair based on background, early environmental influences as well as on current life situation. The individual's balance at the time he encounters a stress situation will largely determine how he will react to that incident.

There are four stages in reacting to stress which overlap and merge with one another. Stage one involves the initial adaptation to the stress situation. Physiological changes occur in the person and he becomes aroused and develops a state of readiness, with heightened receptivity and being *keyed up* for action. This advances into stage two which involves maximum effectiveness.

The individual being keyed up physically and mentally feels self-confident and ready to meet the external stress stimulus. If the stress is overcome quickly at this stage, there is no problem. But if the stress continues over a period of time without actively being overcome, confidence starts giving way and the threat appears to increase. If continued, this merges into stage three which is the hyper-reactive phase.

Despair begins to increase as the stress remains a threat, resulting in increased sensitivity to any possible threatening stimuli. There is a perceptual narrowing at this point and a tendency to interpret many external cues as potential threats which are reacted to quickly by the individual. The danger of indiscriminate and random reactions to a perceived threat are greatly increased during this stage and the individual feels that he would rather act and make a mistake than just continue to endure the stress indefinitely. This could be called the phase of acting-out.

However, the acting-out tends to be a blind, stress-reducing type rather than a goal-directed, constructive kind. Stage four is the end point with emotional exhaustion, being overwhelmed by despair and physical fatigue, and the inability to act.

Although the physiological components involved in stress reactions are somewhat automatic, a policeman can be trained in directing his predictable reactions to stress in a constructive direction congruent with department goals. This kind of training is likely to increase the confidence of the officer. It involves knowledge training, which includes knowledge of himself, the law, his role, and possible outcomes in a variety of typical and recurrent stress situations.

Second, indoctrination training is designed to impact motivations and attitudes and to increase morale by instilling pride and self-confidence, which helps maintain positive balance in subsequent stress situations. The third component is skill training which involves developing a level of proficiency acceptable in performing tasks considered essential to the job.

Finally, practical experience training, perhaps the most important kind, puts the trainee in highly realistic simulated situations where he must actually confront and deal with the stress situation including decision-making and action. Immediate feedback of errors and correct responses coupled with successive retraining until the success level is reached are important.

By repeated exposure to stress situations under controlled conditions and immediate correction of mistakes, the trainee can increase his confidence and familiarity with stress problems which will reduce the implied threat. What is unfamiliar produces higher anxiety than what is familiar.

Some of the research studies indicate that accident-involved drivers tend to have less control of hostility, are more aggressive, more sociable and have lower tension tolerance.[20] Older drivers and females tend to have fewer accidents and traffic violations than their male counterparts. Another study[19] points out that emotional upset contributes to accidents. The individual's skill reactions tend to become disorganized while under emotional stress, and chronic as well as acute emotional states contribute to the frequency of accidents.

Factors which often affect pursuit behavior include aggressive-competitive attitudes and judgment. Men who perceive the pursued as a personal challenge to masculinity and adequacy are more likely to take risks and continue a no-win pursuit to a harmful conclusion. The need to compete with a traffic suspect at high speeds in dangerous circumstances can be compared to being manipulated into a fight by an insecure, provocative person.

Mature officers retain good judgment in the pursuit situation and discontinue the chase when the risks obviously outweigh the possible gain. With reason as well as emotion motivating their behavior, professional officers have better perceptual and cognitive control during the pursuit situation.

Attempts to improve driving behavior should emphasize the driver's understanding of the effect of his personality and emotions on his driving behavior. The goal should be the development of inner controls rather than demanding external controls which the individual isn't responsible for. Driver training programs have to confront psychological and attitudinal variables as well as the usual technical skills.

Overall the evidence suggests that a complex of physiological and psychological factors are involved in driving which are compounded in the stress of high speed pursuit situations.

It has been demonstrated that training which simulates the real event as closely as possible can prepare the officer and allow his success level to be increased in a protected situation while his skills, judgments and behaviors are evaluated. Good driver training programs will include not only the technical aspects of driving, but also the psychological-emotional variables which have the greatest impact on decision-making under stress.

TO SHOOT OR NOT TO SHOOT

The use of deadly force in police work is one of the most emotionally-loaded areas for public and police, with strong feelings being generated on both sides of the issue.

In 1971, 126 law enforcement officers were killed due to criminal action, compared to 100 slain in 1970, 86 in 1969, and 64 in 1968. A total of 122 law enforcement officers were killed in the line of duty from 1962 to 1971.

Since 1962, firearms have been used to commit 96 percent of these police killings, with 73 percent of these being hand guns. Of the 975 offenders known to have been involved in the killing of police officers from the period 1962 to 1971, 77 percent had been arrested previously on some criminal charge, 43 percent had been arrested for a violent crime such as murder, forcible rape, robbery, assault with intent to kill, and 61 percent of those convicted had been granted leniency in the form of parole or probation.

During 1971, approximately nineteen out of every hundred law enforcement officers were assaulted in the line of duty. Of these, 7 percent involved the use of firearms. Assaults resulting in injury totaled an estimated 26,600 while assaults with no injury totaled 48,800. As had occurred in the three previous years, firearms were used to commit 65 percent of the murders during 1971. Since

1966, the use of firearms to commit murder has increased 75 percent and assaults through the use of firearms have increased 109 percent.[8]

There are more policemen slain in the United States than in most other nations. There is no doubt that the danger involved in police work has been steadily increasing.

As a result of an initial survey of shooting reports, two operational changes were initiated in the Los Angeles Police Department in 1971. One was a switch from single-action to double-action shooting. The second was banning the use of small calibre and automatic pistols. These changes were made to reduce the number of accidental, uncontrolled firings in a variety of situations, particularly during searches, pursuits or arrests with drawn weapons.

In single-action shooting a trigger pull of only two pounds was enough to fire the weapon whereas in the double-action mode an eight-pound trigger pull was necessary before the weapon discharged.

A review of the professional literature on decision-making under stress was made and some important physiological factors were noted. However, these physiological changes are not directly related to the individual's ability to use good judgment under stress. They merely heighten his sensitivity to stimuli and get him ready for action.

Physical conditioning plays an important part because of its relationship to fatigue and mental stability. Good physical condition means that an individual does not become tired as quickly and also maintains his positive mental state much longer. The fatigued individual will make poorer judgments under stress, relying on his background of biases and beliefs rather than on objective data. It will affect his shooting accuracy as well.

Although physiological factors are omnipresent, they are usually less crucial than the psychological-emotional variables present in responses to all stress situations which affect decision-making under stress.

The psychological factors can be divided into two basic categories: background factors and situational factors. Background factors are those related to the personality makeup of the individual. Situational factors are created by the stress incident itself.

The background or personality variables involve basic emotional security, self-concept, interpersonal relationships, intelligence, role identity and general emotional maturity.

The initial psychological assessment of police applicants attempts to evaluate the background factors in order to eliminate those who are emotionally and psychologically unsuited to police work. However, this kind of evaluation can only tap the most obvious problems, and still leaves a wide range of personalities and behaviors considered within the normal range.

Additional factors such as morale and value system also contribute to overall reactions to stress. Low morale, an irresponsible attitude, a job assignment considered unimportant, or felt injustices can cause the officer to be less resistant to stress. Temporary maladjustments due to lack of rest, physical illness, financial or marital difficulties, can also influence the individual's behavior in a stress situation.

Situational factors in a stress situation involve basic self-confidence versus insecurity and despair. Despair is the person's reaction to: (a) threat to his personal security, (b) a threat to the goals of the organization he works for, and (c) the threat that he sees to his own self-esteem. Confidence is the person's conviction that he can cope with these threats successfully.

The normal individual operates on a day-to-day basis with a particular balance of confidence and despair based on a complex of early experiences and learned reactions to them. A balance of strong self-confidence and weak despair is most desirable. However, the actual balance that an individual brings to a particular stress situation will help determine how he will react. How people react to stress has been outlined by Selye.[35]

Training can be extremely useful in conditioning officers to stress situation will help determine how he will react. How people to it. By recreating and simulating stress situations as close to the real as possible, training can condition officers to become more resistant to stress. Familiarity tends to reduce anxiety and build confidence. This can be done by a safe repetition of stress situations in a training situation prior to a real life occurrence in the field.

The more successful the officer is in overcoming threat and learning to use good judgment in a training situation, the greater the likelihood that this will carry over into the field. Instructional criticism should be constructive rather than demeaning. Errors should be corrected and reviewed. However, emphasis should be on good performance rather than on the unacceptable.

As part of the knowledge training in shoot, no-shoot situations it is important for officers to understand the legal limits and organizational policies. This will not relieve them of using good judgment and discretion in field situations, but it will provide them with general guidelines. The California Penal Code sections pertaining to justifiable homicides as they relate to police officers include the following:

Homicide is justifiable when committed by public officers and those acting by their command in their aid and assistance, either—

1. In obedience to any judgment of a competent court; or
2. When necessarily committed in overcoming actual resistance to the execution of legal process, or in the discharge of any other legal duty; or
3. When necessarily committed in retaking felons who have been rescued or have escaped, or when necessarily committed in arresting persons charged with committing felony, but who are fleeing from justice or resisting such arrest.

Homicide is also justifiable when committed by any person in any of the following cases:

1. When resisting any attempt to murder any person, or to commit a felony, or to do some great bodily injury upon any person; or,
2. When committed in defense of habitation, property, or person, against one who manifestly intends or endeavors, by violence or surprise, to commit a felony, or against one who manifestly intends and endeavors in a violent, riotous or tumultuous manner, to enter the habitation of another for the purpose of offering violence to any person therein; or,
3. When committed in the lawful defense of such person, or of a wife or husband, parent, child, master, mistress, or servant of such person, when there is reasonable ground to

apprehend a design to commit a felony or to do some great bodily injury, and imminent danger of such design being accomplished; but such person, or the person in whose behalf the defense was made, if he was the assailant or engaged in mutual combat, must really and in good faith have endeavored to decline any further struggle before the homicide was committed; or,

4. When necessarily committed in attempting, by lawful ways and means, to apprehend any person for any felony committed, or in lawfully suppressing any riot, or in lawfully keeping and preserving the peace. Amended.
   Stats. 1963. Chap. 372.

The Los Angeles Police Department Policy Manual includes the following section on shooting:[30]

1. Necessity that officers be armed.

   As long as members of the public are victims of violent crimes and officers in the performance of their duties are confronted with deadly force, it will remain necessary for police officers to be properly armed for the protection of society and themselves.

2. Reason for the use of deadly force.

   An officer is equipped with a firearm to defend himself or others against deadly force or, when it reasonably appears necessary, to effect the arrest of an escaping felon. An officer does not necessarily shoot with the intent to kill; he shoots when it reasonably appears necessary to prevent the individual from completing what he is attempting. When a firearm is used by an officer, it must be with the realization that the death of some person may occur, not necessarily with the intent that such will be the result.

3. Minimizing the risk of death.

   In the extreme stress of a shooting situation, an officer may not have the opportunity or ability to direct his shot to a non-fatal area. To require him to do so in every instance, could increase the risk of harm to himself or others. However, in keeping with the philosophy that the minimum force that reasonably appears necessary should be used, officers should be aware that, even in the rare cases where the use of firearms reasonably appears necessary, the risk of death to any person should be minimized.

4. JUSTIFICATION LIMITED TO FACTS KNOWN TO OFFICER.

Justification for the use of deadly force must be limited to what reasonably appear to be the facts known or perceived by an officer at the time he decides to shoot. Facts unknown to an officer, no matter how compelling, cannot be considered in later determining whether the shooting was justified.

5. SELF DEFENSE AND DEFENSE OF OTHERS.

The law of justifiable homicide authorizes an officer to use deadly force when it reasonably appears necessary to protect himself or others from what reasonably appears as an immediate threat of great bodily harm or from imminent peril of death. The policy of the Department does not limit that law.

6. FLEEING FELONS.

By statute, an officer is authorized the use of deadly force when it reasonably appears necessary to prevent the escape of a felon. Such force may only be exercised when all reasonable alternatives have been exhausted and must be based only on facts or what reasonably appear to be the facts known to the officer at the moment he shoots.

It is not practical to enumerate specific felonies and state with certainty that the escape of the perpetrator must be prevented at all costs, or that there are other felonious crimes where the perpetrator must be allowed to escape rather than to shoot him. Such decisions are based upon sound judgment, not arbitrary checklists.

7. JUVENILE FELONY SUSPECTS.

An officer generally should not shoot at a fleeing felon whom he has reasonable grounds to believe is a juvenile.

However, when the escape of such a suspect can reasonably be expected to pose a serious threat to the life of another person, then under these circumstances an officer may shoot to prevent the escape of such person. This section does not limit an officer's right of self-defense or his defense of others whose lives he reasonably believes are in imminent peril.

8. SHOOTING AT FLEEING MISDEMEANANTS.

Officers may not intentionally use deadly force to effect the arrest or prevent the escape of a misdemeanant.

9. FIRING WARNING SHOTS.

Generally, warning shots should not be fired in an attempt to induce the surrender of a suspect.

10. HOSTAGES.

Criminals who use hostages to effect their escape are desperate individuals who, if allowed to escape, will pose a continuing threat to their hostage and to the public at large. Assurance that a hostage will be released unharmed is a meaningless promise. The Department does not have the ability to protect the safety of a hostage who is allowed to be removed from the presence of officers. The safety of hostages can be best assured by keeping them in the presence of officers and by preventing their removal by the suspect. Officers should use every verbal and tactical tool at their disposal to secure the arrest of the suspect without harming the hostage. However, officers should realize that exceptional situations could arise where considered judgment might dictate allowing removal of a hostage, such as where there is imminent and probable danger to a large group of persons.

11. OFFICERS SURRENDERNG WEAPON.

An officer or his partner may be at the mercy of an armed suspect who has the advantage, but experience has shown that the danger to an officer is not reduced by his giving up his gun upon demand. Surrendering his weapon might mean giving away his only chance for survival; therefore, an officer should use every tactical tool at his disposal to avoid surrendering his weapon.

12. BARRICADED SUSPECTS.

A. *Tactical Plan:* A barricaded suspect poses an extreme danger not only to officers who seek to arrest him, but to other persons as well. Good judgment demands that a tactical plan be developed rather than immediately rushing a barricaded suspect.

Officers should seal avenues of escape and call for assistance. Once the suspect is isolated, time is to the benefit of the officers, and the full resources of the Department are available to assist officers in removing the suspect from his location. To minimize the possibility of injury to officers and others appropriate special equipment and trained personnel should be requested as needed. If possible, an effort should be made to contact the suspect in an attempt to persuade him to voluntarily surrender before force is used.

B. *Supervision at scene of barricaded suspect:* When a suspect is located as the result of a follow-up investigation, the senior investigative officer at the scene is in command. In situations which develop from radio calls or spontaneous activities, the senior uniformed officer present is in command.

The following is a suggested procedure which has been used successfully by the LAPD in shooting situations involving injury or death.

A. AT THE SCENE:

1. Immediately notify Communications Division, apprise them of the situation and request a sergeant, an ambulance, and the detectives. Use judgment in how you make this notification.

2. Even though injured, suspects shall be handcuffed un-

less they have obviously expired, or until it has been determined that they are no longer armed, no longer a threat to others, and no longer capable of escape.

3. Take the necessary steps to preserve the scene.
4. Notify your watch commander as soon as possible.
5. A sergeant will cause you to be transported from the scene to the station as soon as practicable.

B. *At the Station:*

1. A sergeant will be with you during any interviews you may have.
2. Make certain your reports are factual and coincide with the physical evidence.
3. You will be interviewed by Robbery-Homicide Division, geographic investigators, and possibly Internal Affairs Division.
4. You wll be interviewed by your captain and/or the Operations Duty Officer.
5. You will be temporarily assigned to non-field duties.

C. LATER:

1. Your shooting will be reviewed by the Department Shooting Review Board.
2. If the shooting is not justifiable, you may be charged by a criminal court or grand jury.
3. There is also the possibility the case will be reviewed by Federal officials for possible violation of civil rights.

D. ADDITIONAL INFORMATION:

1. Possible verdicts of the coroner's jury include:
   A. Natural
   B. Suicide
   C. Accidental
   D. At the hands of another person
2. The Department Shooting Review Board is comprised of:
   A. The Commanding Officer, Personnel and Training Bureau, as Chairman.

B. The bureau commanding officer of the involved employee.
C. The division commanding officer of the involved employee.
D. The Commanding Officer, Training Division, as ex officio member.
3. Possible findings of the Shooting Review Board are:
A. In policy
B. In policy—substandard
C. Accidental
D. Out of policy

The Los Angeles Police Department Manual requires that an officer who discharges a firearm must notify the Investigative Headquarters Division. This includes all shootings; hit or miss, on or off duty, in or out of the City.

Investigation and reporting of the circumstances of a shooting in which the officer or suspect is shot will be conducted by Robbery-Homicide Division, officer-involved shooting team. Concerned geographic investigators are responsible for the completion of the arrest and crime reports. If neither a suspect or officer is shot then the circumstances of the shooting will be investigated and reported by the involved officers' supervisor.

BIBLIOGRAPHY

1. Bard, Morton: *Training Police As Specialists in Family Crisis Intervention.* Law Enforcement Assistance Administration, 1970.
2. Bard, Morton and Zacker, Joseph: The prevention of family violence: Dilemmas of community intervention. *Journal of Marriage and the Family,* November, 1971, pp. 677-682.
3. Barocas, Harvey and Katz, Myron: Dayton's pilot training program: Crisis intervention. *The Police Chief,* July, 1971, pp. 20-26.
4. Birdwhistell, Ray L.: *Kinesics and Context.* Philadelphia, U of Pa Pr, 1970.
5. *Campus Tensions: Analysis and Recommendations.* American Council on Education, 1970.
6. *Civil Disturbances and Disasters.* FM 19-15, Headquarters, Department of the Army, March, 1968.

7. Coates, Joseph: *Wit and Humor: A Neglected Aid in Crowd and Mob Control.* Institute for Defense Analysis, June, 1970.
8. *Crime Control Digest,* August 25, 1972, pp. 9-10.
9. Dudycha, G. J.: *Psychology for Law Enforcement Officers.* Springfield, Thomas, 1970.
10. Epstein, C.: *Intergroup Relations for Police Officers.* Baltimore, Williams and Wilkens, 1962.
11. Flammang, C. J.: *The Police and the Underprotected Child.* Springfield, Thomas, 1970.
12. Fleishman, Alfred: *Sense and Nonsense—A Study in Human Communication.* International Society for General Semantics, 1971.
13. Gil, David: Violence against children. *Journal of Marriage and the Family,* November, 1971, pp. 637-648.
14. Giovannoni, Jeanne: Parental mistreatment: Perpetrators and victims. *Journal of Marriage and the Family,* November, 1971, pp. 649-657.
15. Glaser, E. M.: *A Program to Train Police Officers to Intervene in Family Disturbances.* Final LEAA Report. Human Inter-Action Research Institute, 1970.
16. Helfer, Roy and Kempe, C. Henry: *The Battered Child.* Chicago, U of Chicago Pr, 1968.
17. Johnson, Paula and Sears, David: *Black Invisibility and the Watts Riot.* Western Psychological Association Convention, Vancouver, June, 1969.
18. Knapp, Vrinda S.: *The Role of the Juvenile Police in the Protection of Neglected and Abused Children.* Ann Arbor, Univ Microfilms, 1967.
19. Malfetti, James: Human behavior—factor X. *Annals of the American Academy of Political and Social Science,* November, 1958, pp. 93-102.
20. McBride, Robin: Prediction of driving behavior following a group driver training session. *Journal of Applied Psychology,* 1970, Vol. 54, pp. 45-50.
21. *Mental Illness and Law Enforcement.* Law Enforcement Study Center, Washington University, 1970.
22. *Miami Report.* The Report of the Miami Study Team on Civil Disturbances in Miami, Florida during the week of August 5, 1968. U.S. Government Printing Office, January 15, 1969.
23. *Model Civil Disturbance Control Plan.* Los Angeles Police Department, March, 1968.
24. Momboisse, Raymond: *Crowd Control and Riot Prevention.* Department of Justice, State of California, 1964.
25. *Operational Guidelines—Community Tensions and Civil Disturbances.* International Association of Chiefs of Police, July, 1967.
26. *Pursuit in Traffic Law Enforcement.* Traffic Institute, Northwestern University, 1967.

27. *1967 Emergency Operations Symposium.* System Development Corporation, April, 1968.
28. Phelps, Lourn, et al.: Training an entire patrol division in domestic crisis intervention techniques. *The Police Chief,* July, 1971, pp. 18-19.
29. *Police Response to Family Disputes.* A Training Manual for Family Crisis Intervention. New York Police Department, 1969.
30. *Policy—The Department Manual, Volume I.* Los Angeles Police Department, March, 1972.
31. *Relieving the Burden of the Mentally Ill on Law Enforcement Agencies* (a grant proposal). Enki Corporation, January, 1971.
32. Roland, Loyd and Matthews, Robert: *How to Recognize and Handle Abnormal People.* National Association of Mental Health, 1964.
33. Schultz, Donald O.: *Special Problems in Law Enforcement.* Springfield, Thomas, 1971.
34. Schultz, J. H. and Luthe, W.: *Autogenic Training.* New York, Grune, 1959.
35. Selye, Hans: *The Stress of Life.* New York, McGraw, 1956.
36. Siegel, A. et al: *Professional Police-Human Relations Training.* Springfield, Thomas, 1963.
37. Speigel, John: *The Group Psychology of Campus Disorders—A Transactional Approach.* Lemberg Center for the Study of Violence, Brandeis University, 1970.
38. Speigel, John: *Race Relations and Violence—A Social Psychiatric Perspective.* Presented at Association for Research in Nervous and Mental Diseases, New York, December 1, 1967.
39. Speigel, John: Psychosocial factors in riots—old and new. *American Journal of Psychiatry,* September, 1968, pp. 281-285.
40. Speigel, John: *Toward a Theory of Collective Violence.* Lemberg Center for the Study of Violence, Brandeis University, 1968.
41. Spitz, Rene: *The First Year of Life.* New York, Intl Univs Pr, 1965.
42. Watson, N. A.: *Police-Community Relations.* International Association of Chiefs of Police, 1966.
43. Wilson, Jerry: Demonstrations and police. *National Police Journal.* Winter, 1972, pp. 2-5.
44. *Words Make a Difference.* New York Police Department, 1967.
45. Younger, Evelle: *The Battered Child.* District Attorney's Information Pamphlet Number 2, County of Los Angeles, 1970.

CHAPTER TEN

DEVELOPING POTENTIAL
AND PERSONAL GROWTH

WE ARE USUALLY our own worst enemies. We put on hand-cuffs and chains and make ourselves prisoners of suspicion, fear, illness, routine boredom and unhappiness. Most of us operate on only two to four cylinders out of eight because we don't feel worthwhile, deserving or talented because of subconscious nag-gings of inadequacy and inferiority. We plod along in a dull rou-tine, victims of habit. But the potential for achievement, creativity and innovation are there. They merely have to be unlocked from the restraints we have imprisoned them with. The problem is basically one of self-concept.

SELF-ASSESSMENT

Taking a hard look at one's self is the first step in the evaluation process. Questions to be asked include, Who am I? What am I worth? Am I really an independent functioning adult? Am I standing on my own two feet with inner security and self-confi-dence, or am I loaded with anxiety and fear, feeling helpless and childlike? Do I worry too much about what other people think rather than what I value?

An examination of one's value system, beliefs and attitudes is important since they strongly influence what we think and do. What kinds of things should have priority in the individual's value system? Where should his wife rate on the totem pole? How does she rate compared to the job, to the children, to parents, to the car, to fishing trips?

The man who tries to maintain the double standard in order

to bolster his own sense of superiority usually has considerable doubt and anxiety about his own adequacy as a male. The secure male is able to view females as equal human beings. He is capable of developing a relationship with a female on a non-sexual basis rather than relating to every female as an object of conquest.

Another aspect of the self-system that needs to be assessed involves the whole question of goals. Where am I headed in life? What are my objectives? The individual without goals is rudderless. He drifts along aimlessly, living each day at a time rather than working to achieve greater future satisfaction.

The police officer who doesn't know where he is going in the police department is most frequently the individual who does not get promoted, who feels that he is a victim of the organization, and who tends to look forward to retirement as a sort of blissful state which will allow him to achieve happiness and success. However, this is likely to be a cruel illusion if no long range goals have been developed.

Retirement for many men constitutes a trap which strips away part of one's identification, sense of importance, contribution to self, and to society, and the feeling of usefulness in general.[6] The achieving individual does not place too high a value on retirement because he gets such great satisfaction out of his vocation self. He is constantly thinking of ways to broaden himself, to achieve in his work, to make himself a more effective professional. His main motives are self-satisfaction and self-esteem.

The truly adult individual is a highly ethical creature who has great regard for fellow human beings of all types. He tends to be honest and sensitive to the needs of others. His high ethical sense is based on his own internal value system rather than on the fear of punishment or fear of exposure. His sense of self-worth also obviates the need for any deviousness. He desires to remain open, open to new ideas, to new learning and to the change accompanying growth.

LEARNING—THE OPEN MIND

One of the dangers to the new young policeman is developing tunnel vision. This involves seeing things as either black or white, good people or bad people. A close-minded attitude is much easier to maintain because it requires less expenditure of thought and energy.

If one maintains fixed beliefs, there is no need to re-examine one's feelings and ideas. Self-examination is a painful, effort-consuming process. However, very quickly the close-minded individual gets to be an anachronism. He is out of touch with the current state of affairs in the world and with what is happening in society. Consequently, he tends to feel more alone, apart and isolated himself. This increases the distance he feels between himself and other people.

The close-minded individual tends to dislike himself and other people as well. He is pessimistic, cynical, depressed, authoritarian and heavy-minded in his approach to people unlike himself, especially minority groups. He often goes through life feeling that other people are trying to victimize him, that he's getting *the short end of the stick*.

An open mind is accessible to ideas, feelings, attitudes, and to other belief systems. It has the ability to deal with ambiguity and dissonance, and to see them as socially desirable and healthy. Not every complex issue can be reduced to simple terms. Complexity and ambiguity are facts of life.

The mature individual learns how to tolerate and cope rather than run away, deny, or over-simplify. He tends to see himself as a life-long student, with learning beginning at birth and continuing until death. No one can possibly know or can learn everything, since knowledge is constantly being generated and old *truths* are being modified and discarded over time.

An attitude of openness includes curiosity, a desire for involvement, inquisitiveness, and some healthy skepticism. The open-minded individual likes people, enjoys what life has to offer and sees new experiences as an interesting challenge and adventure rather than something to be afraid of. He looks forward to each day and to the future with pleasure and optimism, feeling that people and life are worthwhile.

There appears to be a positive correlation between formal education and open-mindedness. This suggests that college training, particularly learning in humanities, social and behavioral sciences, has a tendency to open one's mind, present new facts and ideas, and to help a person grow. The old time officer who denigrates formal education and views college graduates as soft is trying to cling to a bygone era. The days of valuing brawn rather than brain in police work are past.

ACHIEVEMENT MOTIVATION

In order to achieve, one must be motivated, have a need to construct, to work, to contribute.

Most people who achieve at a high level are self-motivated and self-actualizing.[12] The desire to achieve can spring from various levels within the personality.

One is an early childhood desire of wanting to prove to overly critical parents that one is really good, capable and intelligent. This motive rests on a kind of *I'll prove it to them* need. At another level the achievement motive may be based on identifications with important people in one's life. Identifying with a teacher, a boss, a relative, some ideal figure that one desires to emulate, becomes very important in shaping the direction of one's achievement.

At still another level one's motive to achieve may result from a fusion of the various needs that are synthesized within the self-concept. This includes a value system that has been welded together after discarding undesirable or unusable values from the past, so that the new value system becomes a highly personal, independent set of beliefs, attitudes and goals.

Some research in the area of achievement motivation has suggested that high achievement motivation is related to the intensity of training for independence in childhood. The child who is forced to be on his own very early will have a need to accomplish.

The fathers of those scoring high on achievement motivation were perceived as unfriendly and unhelpful, while the mothers of the same children were more demanding for achievement at early ages than were the mothers of low achievers.[8]

One of the complicating factors in the whole area of achievement motivation is that frequently motives are unconscious in nature and outside of one's awareness and control. This can be a problem if there are additional underlying conflicts within the personality that require large amounts of energy resulting in preoccupation, fatigue, and the inability to confront external reality.

In extreme cases of neurotic conflict, counseling or psychotherapy can be very useful in resolving the underlying problems and freeing the trapped energy for use in more constructive, external pursuits. There is some evidence that job satisfaction is the best predictor of longevity. Neff[15] provides an interesting discussion of the components of the work personality as related to achievement.

CREATIVITY, INNOVATION AND ORIGINALITY

The creative process involves freedom and restrictions. It is a search for a new experience or a new object not easily obtainable, a search that is never actually completed.

What are some of the characteristics of creative individuals? Traits identified with eminent creators are divergent thinking, intelligence, intrinsic task involvement and preference for complexity.[15] Hard work and dedication are also important ingredients of achievement.

Eminent people function independently and rely on their own ideas and their own evaluation of them. They also have a high level of commitment to their work, and a need for quality and novelty in creative achievement.[2]

Highly creative people tend to see authority as conventional rather than absolute. They make fewer black and white distinctions and have a less dogmatic, more relativistic view of life. They are more independent in judgment, less conventional and conforming intellectually and socially, more willing to entertain, place a value on humor and are freer and less rigid in their behavior.[11]

Gough[8] lists some characteristics of creative thinking which include flexibility, unique individual associations, concern for form and elegance. Underlying personality and motivational traits include intellectual competence, an inquiring mind, flexibility, esthetic sensitivity and a sense of destiny.

Although innovation and originality appear to be related to creativity, they are precursors of creative achievement. Creativity involves independent functioning and self-motivated curiosity and achievement, but it also includes other people. A work or production may be original and satisfy oneself, but may not necessarily be creative. The creative effort adds something to what has existed previously. It has not merely rearranged the same old forms to the base of the original parts.

The process of creativity occurs in stages, some conscious, some unconscious which unfold slowly or rapidly in succeeding phases until finally, there is synthesis in some achievement, a work of art, a project or an invention.

In artistic achievement, the individual can use his unconscious, primary processes without eliminating abstractions. By having access to his unconscious impulses, symbols and images, the individual utilizes them as inputs for abstracting conscious new forms or new ideas which were not possible before.

The work of art appeals to the unconscious symbolism and imagery in people. It is perceived as an enriching experience by the viewer who is sharing in the creative process by identifying with it and having his own primary processes stirred and captured in a conscious art form.[1]

PERSISTENCE AND SUCCESS

The secret to success is persistence. Although some basic talent is usually required, the main ingredient is the ability to stick with a program or project long enough to overcome the various obstacles that always abound. From candidates for Ph.D. degrees to policemen desiring to advance in police organizations, tenacity is required for success. However, in order to persist, the individual must feel that he has something to contribute, that he is worthwhile and should succeed.

If he is ambivalent about whether he really deserves promotion or success in an endeavor, he will probably sabotage himself in order to fail. If one operates on a *script* of inferiority, unworthiness and a need for failure, then the persistent effort that one puts forth will eventuate in failure since this would be the underlying need and motive.[3]

Success should be based on personal qualities related to one's self-image. If success is equated solely with the acquiring of material goods, there is the likelihood that it will never be attained in sufficient quantity. When success is based on self-worth and inner security, the influence on behavior of external objects and other people diminishes.

The person having his own value system functions as an equal independent adult, and relies on his own assessments and beliefs in determining whether he is successful. Some external praise and reward are necessary and desirable, but should merely reinforce an all ready well-founded sense of competence and worth.

The successful professional policeman will function using his own value system rather than that of his peers. He will view himself as an independently functioning adult who is equal to any other adult, in his organization or in the world. He will not be in awe of authority, titles or trappings, and will see other individuals as human beings regardless of their station in life, or the amount of money or possessions they may have.

The individual who feels truly worthwhile will persist because he feels that he has a right to achieve his goals and is willing to work toward them.

BIBLIOGRAPHY

1. Arieti, Silvano: *The Intrapsychic Self.* New York, Basic, 1967.
2. Barron, Frank: *Creativity and Personal Freedom.* New York, Van N-Rein, 1968.
3. Berne, Eric: *What Do You Say After You Say Hello?* New York, Grove, 1972.
4. Blalock, Joyce: Civil liability of officers. *FBI Law Enforcement Bulletin,* February, 1972.
5. Cattell, Raymond B. and Butcher, H.: *The Prediction of Achievement and Creativity.* New York, Bobbs, 1968.
6. Cooley, Leland F. and Lee, M.: *The Retirement Trap.* Garden City, Doubleday, 1965.
7. Gardner, John W.: *Self Renewal: The Individual and the Innovative Society.* New York, Harp T., 1964.
8. Gough, Harrison: Identifying the creative man. *Journal of Value Engineering,* 1964, 2, pp. 5-12.
9. Haefele, J.: *Creativity and Innovation.* Reinhold, 1962.
10. Kagen, Jerome (ed.): *Creativity and Learning.* Boston, HM, 1967.
11. McKinnon, Donald W.: Personality and the realization of creative potential. *American Psychologist,* 1965, 20, pp. 273-281.
12. Maslow, Abraham: *The Farther Reaches of Human Nature.* New York, Viking Pr, 1971.

13. McClelland, David C.: *The Achieving Society*. New York, Van N-Rein, 1961.
14. Mills, Robert: Education Strategies for Police in a Community Services College. Presented at American Psychological Association Convention, September, 1971.
15. Neff, Walter S.: *Work and Human Behavior*. New York, Atherton, 1968.
16. Nicholls, John: Creativity in the person who will never produce anything original and useful: The concept of creativity as a normally distributed trait. *American Psychologist,* Vol. 27, August, 1972, pp. 717-727.
17. Selye, Hans: *In Vivo*. New York, Liveright, 1967.
18. Stein, M. and Heinze, S. (eds.): *Creativity and the Individual: Summaries of Selected Literature in Psychology and Psychiatry*. New York, Free Pr, 1960.
19. Vernon P. (ed.): *Creativity: Selected Readings*. Baltimore, Penguin, 1970.

NAME INDEX

SUBJECT INDEX

Accident, 114
Accident prone, 141
Acting-out, 139, 143
Acting-out behavior, 19
Acting-out is anti-social, 97
Activity, 49
Addiction, 100 (*see also* Alcohol,
    Amphetamines, Barbiturates,
    Cocaine, Hallucinogens,
    Hashish, Heroin, Marijuana)
Addictions, 61 (*see also* Drug Addic-
    tions)
Adult situational reaction, 61
Affective reactions, 62
Aggression, 25, 92
Aggressive-competitive attitudes, 144
Aggressive impulses, 63
Alcohol, 21, 97, 98 (*see also* Addic-
    tion, Drinking excessively,
    Drugs)
Alcoholism, 21, 99
Ambivalence, 64
American Automobile Association,
    141
Amphetamines, 100 (*see also* Addic-
    tion Drugs)
Anal, 96
Angry and uncontrolled disciplinary
    response, 133
Anomie, 89
Anonymity, 139
Anticipatory anxiety, 57
Anti-social behavior, 114
Anti-social reaction, 61
Anxiety, 21 (*see also* Anticipatory
    Anxiety reactions)
Anxiety reaction, 60
Assassin, 119
Atherosclerosis, 51 (*see also* Cardio-
    vascular disturbance, Heart
    attacks)

Attitudes, 32, 71, 157
Attitudinal variables, 145
Authoritarian, 123
Authority, 19, 122, 123
Authority symbol, 16
Autonomic nervous system, 142

Bangs, Sgt. John W. III, vii
Barbiturates, 100, 101 (*see also* Ad-
    diction, Drugs)
Barricaded suspects, 152
Battered children, 140
Behavior modification, 106
Behavioral, 109
Behavioral sciences, 3
Behavioral scientists, 105
Beliefs, 157
Blood-alcohol level, 22
Board of Police Commissioners, vii
Board of Rights, 19
Bodily mannerisms, 125
Body ego, 140
Borderline psychotic, 52
Bova, Lt. Jerold M., vii
Broken record syndrome, 64
Budgeting, 23
Burglary, 20
Burrescia, Rachael, vii
Business franchise swindles, 94

California, 29, 131
California Penal Code, 148
Campus demonstration, 137
Cardiovascular disturbance, 51 (*see
    also* Atherosclerosis, Heart
    attacks)
Cardiovascular reactions, 62
Caretaker quarrel, 133
Central Receiving Hospital, 131
Character disorders, 60
Characteristics, 161